Her Story, His Glory

A Series of M.A.D. Conversations™

The Colorfully Candid Paradigm
An Imprint of Candid Liv

An Imprint of Candid Liv
PO Box 335690
North Las Vegas, NV, 89033
www.candidliv.com

Publisher's Note: This is a nonfictional anthology. Some names and identifying details have been changed to protect the privacy of individuals.

Scripture quotations marked CEV are from the Contemporary English Version Copyright © 1991, 1992, 1995 by American Bible Society. Used by Permission.

Scipture quotations marked KJV are from The Bible. Authorized King James Version, Oxford UP, 1998.

Scipture quotations marked MSG are from Peterson, Eugene H. The Message: The Bible in Contemporary Language. NavPress, 2002.

Scipture quotations marked NIV are from The Holy Bible: New International Version. Zondervan, 1984.

Scripture quotations marked NKJV are from Holy Bible: The New King James Version. 1982. Nashville: Thomas Nelson.

Scripture quotations marked NLT *Holy Bible: New Living Translation.* 2015. Carol Stream, IL: Tyndale House Publishers.

Book Layout ©2018 BookDesignTemplates.com

Ordering Information:
Quantity sales. Special discounts are available on quantity purchases by corporations, associations, and others. For details, contact the "Special Sales Department" at the address above.

Her Story, His Glory: A Series of M.A.D. Conversations™ Liv Dooley. -- 1st Ed
ISBN **978-0-9600373-9-1**

Her Story, His Glory: A Series of M.A.D. Conversations™ Liv Dooley. -- 1st Ed
Ebook ISBN **978-0-9600373-8-4**

dedication

We dedicate this book to every child of God into whose hands it falls. We pray that you will find healing and revelation through the testimonies we've shared. We love you.

table of contents

foreword

In 60 years of living as a female, a daughter, a mother, and a mentor, these three things I know for sure: the Lord is good, His mercy is everlasting, and His truth endures to all generations. *His truth endures to all generations.* This last statement is perhaps the most intriguing of them all. Our world is in a constant state of change. Many of our everyday, mundane experiences would have been unimaginable to our parents.

In my own life, there are things I do now that weren't even invented when I was a middle-aged adult. Right now, I am writing the foreword on my phone! How convenient that would have been when I was hand-writing my dissertation 30 years ago because not everyone had a home computer. I am older than color television, microwave ovens, video games, cable, Internet, and cell phones; and I fully understand that the woman or girl who reads this book 30 years from now may have no idea what any of those things are. So, how in the world could God's truth endure to all generations? Maybe because as much as things have changed, many things stay the same. People still populate planet earth. They still need and crave love. They still feel things like hurt, abandonment, fear, pride, perfectionism, loss, unforgiveness, rejection, abuse, and neglect. Women are still daughters, mothers, and mentors. Words still have power. Sin is still causing emotional, physical, social, mental, and relational havoc in the world. People still need God. And because of Him, there is still a world of beautiful things like love, caring, fun, warmth, joy, peace, and true wholeness and contentment. We still have family and friends, and all of that has been going on since the birth of civilization.

The Bible encourages mentorship among women. The elders of the early church asked the older women to teach the younger women the best ways to conduct their lives. People say that experience is the best teacher, and it is. Whatever lessons experience teaches you, trust me, you will learn them very well. However, experience flunks out way too many students. Learning from the experiences of others is a much smarter and less time-consuming way to learn. You get all the benefits of the lesson without having to take the course yourself, saving you time, money, heartache, regret... and maybe even your life.

In this book, you will find all of the things I have shared with you here. You will find the truth that endures to all generations. You will find lessons from girls who are living in the now and lessons from those who have been there, done that, and are wearing the souvenirs in their hearts and minds. You will find some truths that could very well save your life. You don't have to learn everything the hard way. Allow yourself to be mentored and mothered by these stories. You will find that God is good. In spite of every hard thing these women have gone through or that the girls are going through right now, in these pages, you will see that God is good. You will also see that His mercy is everlasting as you walk with them through their transformations. There is victory here. And because this project is multigenerational, you will see how the truth of God transcends generations.

Some of the issues this book addresses are quite sensitive. They may open doors to things that will be difficult for you to handle. You may find yourself having memories triggered, having dreams resurface, or having emotions you're not sure what to do with. If you find yourself more troubled than comforted by the stories in this book, that might be God's way of letting you know that He is ready to start a healing journey with you. Seek a godly counselor or therapist. Don't suffer alone. Don't try to handle it yourself. Remember, experience flunks out lots of students. You may need a little help, and that's okay. I did. Going to therapy was one of the best decisions of my life.

So, enjoy the transformational stories you are about to read. And remember, you have a story of your own. However you decide to walk it out, remember… it's all for His glory.

Dr. Naida M. Parson, PhD

Senior Pastor, New Antioch Christian Fellowship
Owner, A Way With Words
First African American Licensed Psychologist in Nevada

PART ONE

conversations
from a daughter

deception

BY LIV DOOLEY

Why don't you think she's safe? Is it true or is it rooted in a lie or a comparison? I wish I had let her in earlier. Who is she? My mother. I'm not sure why it started, how it started, or when it started. I just remember believing the lies that my mother wasn't any fun, didn't love me, and wasn't on my team or in my corner from a very early age.

Growing up, my mom sent me to the best schools, picked my friends up to take us to church or other outings, sent me on trips for the summer to visit my aunt, and rushed me back and forth to the many extracurriculars and jobs I participated in. In fact, she helped me get my first job and hired all of my friends, too, but instead of focusing on that, I believed the lies that she wasn't any fun, didn't love me, and wasn't on my team or in my corner, and it showed. I was incredibly disrespectful and fully believed I was entitled to the good stuff because the lies had clouded my ability to truly see her.

When I was a senior, my mom insisted on taking me shopping for my prom dress even though she knew I wanted to have it made. Honestly, it confused me that she even wanted to do stuff like that together. I reasoned that she just wanted to show me how much more she knew than me, but she never stopped surprising me. She gave me money for the material when the shopping fell through and she went to every dress fitting I had. I remember looking at her, wondering why she was so cool with the dress that I'd picked out when I wasn't even sure *I* liked it, but I didn't say anything about it. I just continued as usual: quiet, reserved, moody, and nonchalant about her presence.

On the day of the prom, I went about all the regular errands I'd planned as if it was only natural that I do everything alone, but something was different. My mom kept bothering me. She called me a couple of times, wondering where I was, but I gave her vague answers until she showed up at my friend's house, ready to help me dress.

From the moment she arrived, I noticed something was off about her. She was hurried. She was flustered. Was she emotional? Why was this such a big deal to her? After all, I'd believed she wasn't any fun, didn't love me, and wasn't on my team or in my corner. I got ready, and I was surprised by how much she had helped me as we left. That night was disappointingly uneventful, except for the fact that she'd seemed emotional.

A few days later, my dad, who I'm close with, reprimanded me by telling me I should have let my mother in. He told me that prom was something for a mom and a daughter to enjoy together. I sat there, stunned, wondering why. After all, I didn't really think—well, you know the lies by now.

Whether you know that your mom or your mentor loves you or not, I want you to know that what you focus on will magnify. If you focus on all the stuff she does that is different than your friend's mom or all of the things you dislike, you're only going to find more things that you dislike. On the flip side, if you focus on all of the things that she's done to show you how much she loves and cares for you, you'll begin to see that too. First Peter 4:8 says, "Above all, love each other deeply, because love covers over a multitude of sins." Your mom, your bonus mom, your foster mom, your mentor is not going to do everything right; but you can still cover them in love like they continue to cover you in love. Relationships are reciprocal, so let's stop acting out the lie that we're not loved, and start seeing the best in each other.

I'd love to tell you that the conversation with my father changed everything about how I interacted with my mom, but it didn't. Unfortunately, I hid two of the most traumatic events I would ever go through from her after that. I don't want the same for you. John 8:44 tells us that the enemy of our souls—the devil—is the father of lies. I know it's hard to believe that there really is a devil, but he's not the pitchfork-carrying-red-guy who sits on the shoulders of people, influencing them to think funny thoughts. He's much more subtle than that. And somewhere along the way, he made me think my mom didn't love me, even though nothing she did showed that. Yes, she got mad. I stayed on punishment, but that didn't mean that she didn't love me. It actually reinforced her love for me. Hebrews 12:10 tells us that discipline is good for us. Being told no is good for us. Being restricted from doing everything we want to do is good for us. Hebrews 12:11 tells us that even though we don't enjoy it at the time, it produces righteousness and peace in our lives. If there's one thing we need in this world, it's peace. Trust the discipline.

I love spending time with my mother now. She is one of my best friends, but we had to make a lot of strategic steps to get here. We didn't just wake up one day and feel friendly. We had to learn how to communicate, invite one another into our thoughts, and pray together. I know that this may be uncomfortable for you right now and you may not want to read this book with your mom or your mentor, but I'm begging you to let her in! Please, little sis, don't shut her out. If the relationship is beyond repair at this point, I want to invite you to share this time with another big sister, a mentor, an aunt, or a teacher who will love you through this time and pray for your future as if she were your mother. We are here for you.

1 PETER 4:8 NIV

Above all, love each other deeply, because love covers over a multitude of sins.

THOUGHTS TO CONSIDER

1. On a scale from 1 to 10, with 1 being distant and 10 being incredibly close, how close would you say you and your mom/mentor or you and your daughter are? (Write the number down secretly and then reveal it to one another at the same time.)
2. Can you share a few reasons why you answered that way?
3. Are there any lies that you've begun to believe about your relationship like I did?
4. What are some suggestions that you can make to grow closer or maintain the strength of your relationship?

A PRAYER FOR YOU

Dear God,

In the name of Jesus, I thank You for Your wisdom. You chose to give me the mama and mentor I have for such a time as this. I ask, Lord God, that You help me to express my gratitude for those relationships above any concerns or complaints that I may have. I know that what I focus on will magnify, so help me to focus on the good things, the areas of growth I see in myself, and the truth in Your Word. I pray that You would help me to accept the redirection our parents offer and that, in turn, You open the lines of communication so that we may understand each other more deeply.

Bless this time and breathe healing into my emotions as You renew my mind with every chapter that I read and every moment I spend. I am trusting You, Holy Spirit, to speak into every emotion I have, every fear I may hide, and every dream I hold. You are a good, good Father, and I choose to believe that You know what's best for me in every way. Help me to experience Your will and draw me closer in Your presence.

In Jesus' name I pray, amen.

ADDITIONAL SCRIPTURES ON TRUTH

Proverbs 12:22, John 14:6, John 8:32, Ephesians 6:14, Ephesians 4:15, 1 Corinthians 13:4-6, Philippians 4:8

THOUGHTS, PRAYERS, & CONVERSATIONS I NEED TO HAVE

_____

_____

_____

_____

_____

_____

_____

_____

_____

_____

_____

_____

_____

_____

_____

_____

_____

misunderstanding

BY DECEMBER JAMES

From age nine to sixteen I didn't have a positive or realistic view of my mom. Marriage, divorce, single parenting, homelessness, college student, and welfare were all identifiers in our home while I was growing up. My sisters and I were there to witness it all as spectating rag dolls.

We lived with so many people that I lost count around thirteen years old. It didn't even matter because around twelve, I mentally withdrew from my situation. There's very little I can recall from that season. It's like I lived in another world, another dimension. I had to disassociate from my reality because I feared losing all the good that had been placed in me from birth. The good stuff represented the ability to respect myself and others, achieve goals, use my brain to make wise, logical decisions, and the belief that Jesus really does save. All these things were poured into me and I had to protect and shield them before the world violently stripped me of them.

It was graduation day and I wasn't even seventeen yet. I was angry at Mom, yet again, for something she had done wrong, from my birth to that day. She was the only person to blame and always the reason for my anger. I remember asking myself, "Why am I so angry with Mom?" I had never asked myself this question, nor had anyone else. I'm glad, because I never had a logical response.

Fast forward a few years. It's graduation day again. I'm twenty-four years old and looking at my mother again. But this time, my anger towards Mom had decreased because my understanding had increased. Six years and another graduation later—this time for my master's degree—I remember calling Mom before walking across the stage to thank her. Because by then, my anger was just small embers that were being suffocated by my increased understanding of how my childhood had prepared me for such a time as this. You see, my life from the ages nine to sixteen, I just did not have understanding. And at twenty-four, I still didn't get it.

There's a proverb that says, "With all thy getting, get understanding." How could a nine-year-old have an understanding of adult matters? Could it be that I was actually angry at something I lacked the developmental maturity to understand? Let's face it: what does a twelve-year-old really know about being a single parent of three daughters trying to attend college, while facing homelessness? Nothing. At that time in my life, I did not want to be homeless, I did not want to lose my friends, and I wanted my own room with a TV and a PlayStation.

So why did I call my mom to thank her as I received my master's degree? Understanding. I regret that it took so long for me to understand my mom's sacrifices. Yes, she got divorced, but now I understand my father's abusive and destructive nature was not good for my future. Yes, we moved from place to place, but my mom did all she could to protect her daughters from drugs and sex offenders. Mom hauled us across a university campus during the Phoenix summer heat because she could not find babysitters, but she had exams that couldn't be rescheduled. And yes, my mom stayed, even when I was that angry teenager at the high school graduation, wishing her as far away from me as possible. She was there even though I just did not understand.

Today, I am a young mother. I have birth children, adopted children, and foster children in my life, and I realize they also don't understand all of the adult decisions and mistakes that have impacted their lives. They frequently express their anger towards me because of the adult choices that have caused them to live with strangers, form new familial bonds, go to new schools, and start new routines. Just like you, there are some circumstances and events in your life that were left unexplained and misunderstood, and your response was anger. Can it be that you need to get an understanding?

PROVERBS 4:7 NKJV

Wisdom is the principal thing; Therefore get wisdom. And in all your getting, get understanding.

THOUGHTS TO CONSIDER

Before misunderstood anger strips you of your future relationships, get an understanding.

1. Write down two moments or events in your life where you just did not understand it or still don't get it.
2. Anger is a normal human emotion. How you cope and deal with that anger is what's important. With a mentor or your mom, list the things you do when you get angry. Then, determine if they are healthy behaviors. If they are not healthy, find two new healthy behaviors to replace the two negative behaviors. Some positive behaviors are practicing deep breathing, prayer, and taking a walk.

A PRAYER FOR YOU

Heavenly Father,

You see me. You see my anger, the pain, and parts of my life I simply don't understand. You said You knew me when You formed me in my mother's womb and that You had plans for me, not to harm me, so I am asking that You give me understanding today of those plans and my purpose. As I ask for understanding,

God I ask that You heal the anger I am holding towards my mother, help me to release it in order to have the loving relationship I desire to have with my mother. Guide us and direct us to have a moment where we are able to talk and get an understanding together. God, I know You hear me and I thank You in advance for the healing and understanding You are sending.

In the name of Jesus I pray, amen.

ADDITIONAL SCRIPTURES ON UNDERSTANDING

Proverbs 3:5, 1 Kings 3:9, 2 Timothy 3:1-17, Proverbs 14:29, 1 Corinthians 2:12, 2 Timothy 2:7

THOUGHTS, PRAYERS, & CONVERSATIONS I NEED TO HAVE

_____

_____

_____

_____

_____

_____

_____

_____

_____

_____

_____

_____

_____

_____

_____

_____

_____

_____

foolishness

BY SHEILA V. GARDNER

Have you ever felt like you weren't enough? Smart enough, pretty enough, tall enough, loved enough? Would you admit that you tend to judge your self-worth based on the things you see or hear on social media, TV, or music? If you answered yes to either question, then you are not alone! We have all compared ourselves to others on some level.

I remember when my daughter was in middle school and was asked this question: Would you rather be famous or well known? Her response was, "If you're famous, it's usually because of something that you did, good or bad. Fame can make you turn into someone who you don't recognize! But, if you're well-known, people just know you because of *who* you are. You don't have to do anything out of character!"

You see, even at this young age, she possessed a measure of inherent wisdom that was already alive and active inside of her. In a world that focuses on physical appearance, materialism, and personal success, we all face the challenges of combating the myths our culture feeds us and the appetite that it builds within us. We live in a social media era that makes us unconsciously measure our own self-worth. Popularity is based upon likes, comments, and the amount of "followers" we have. Just think about it. People often post themselves at their best and fail to show the behind-the-scenes, unpleasant, confused, chaotic, and doubtful moments. We only see what they want us to see, which is the final, perfected, and edited product. This should help you realize that you are often judging yourself based on someone else's Photoshopped reality.

When we keep God at the forefront of our minds, we will be protected from the tricks, strategies, and schemes that the world tries to win us with. We will also experience protection from an assembly line of regrets. We will remember that He (Jesus) is what is most important in life, and our relationship with Him will last. The fame, pleasure, or attention won't last, but our relationship with Him will. Remember, we are daughters of the King, and we have value because God says we do! He loves us so much that He sent Jesus, His only Son, to die for us so that we could be with Him forever! Allow the love of God to be your confidence and your strength. You cannot give others the power to manipulate and devalue your self-worth. They're not worth it. When we build on a strong foundation, we can resist what the world has to offer! Ask God what He is saying about you. You are beautiful in every way, and there's no flaw in you! Just imagine, God made you one-of-kind. You are an original and not a copy! He blessed you with a specific hair type, skin color, eye color, and a personality that is distinctively yours!

When you learn to embrace your true identity at an early age, you will soar in a level of God-given confidence that will sustain you. This level of confidence is meant to push you toward an entirely different lifestyle—one built around Jesus Christ (not social media). When you encounter Jesus in a personal and life-changing way, He transforms you from the inside out. No matter your age or season in life, obtaining Godly wisdom gives you vision and equips you with the practical tools to live life out LOUD!

It is essential to establish a relationship of wisdom and build on a strong foundation so that you can resist what the world has to offer as you ultimately seek the true definition of beauty, by understanding God's love for you. Proverbs 3:15 (CEV) says, "Wisdom is more valuable than precious jewels; nothing you want compares with her!"

When you allow God's confidence to lead you instead of choosing to live your life through the lens of comparison, you can pursue the ultimate crown of wisdom. When you accomplish this, you will experience a new awakening of purpose. When you choose to implement your weapon of wisdom, you discover the inherent value and worth of who you are in Christ! When we embrace an important reality to ensure our inside thoughts and feelings mirror the time we put into our appearance, we remember that that's what really matters most to God! Therefore, obtaining wisdom is more valuable, and it is everlasting, even when beauty fades. You are destined to receive a triple portion: the crown of *beauty*, the crown of *worth*, and the crown of *wisdom*! You will understand and embrace who you are, why you are called, and what you are predestined to do when you receive that crown. Remember, no one else can do what you were made to do, but you! It...Will Be Worth It!

PROVERBS 3:15 NIV

Wisdom is more valuable than precious jewels; nothing you want compares with her.

THOUGHTS TO CONSIDER

1. What is your personal definition of self-worth?
2. What is something that you love about yourself?
3. How do you balance reality in the midst of media messages?
4. Are you confident in hearing God's voice about your self-worth?

A PRAYER FOR YOU

Father God,

Please diminish the myth that I am invisible and that no one cares! You have given me the power to tread over any attack that the enemy tries to place in my path. God, as I encounter every foul spirit, please provide me with Your strength and let the spirit of peace guard my heart and mind. Please remove depression, low self-esteem, pressures of comparison, unforgiveness, and generational curses. God please provide me with Your comfort and hold me when I feel lonely and afraid.

Please build my confidence and allow me to make clear and intentional choices. Show me how to use my voice, mind, and social platform for Your glory!

Please remove the spirit of confusion and any negative or selfish thoughts from my mind. Show me how to communicate and share my feelings and emotions during difficult and uncertain times. When people fail my expectations, show me that You will always be my friend and You will never leave or forsake me! Bind the spirit of doubt and help me realize that You have made me uniquely smart, beautiful, perfect, and gifted. When people question my worth, value, and importance, please help me to remember that I am enough because You gave up everything for me! Father God, please sow Your wisdom into my heart and mind as I study Your Word. I am a daughter of the King and I have value because You say that I do! Thank You for showering me with Your overwhelming, reckless, never-ending love.

In Jesus' name we pray, amen.

ADDITIONAL SCRIPTURES ON WISDOM

Psalm 111:10, James 1:5, Proverbs 3:13-18, Luke 21:15, James 3:17, Ephesians 1:17

THOUGHTS, PRAYERS, & CONVERSATIONS I NEED TO HAVE

_____

_____

_____

_____

_____

_____

_____

_____

_____

_____

_____

overachieving

BY CHRISTIAN CASHELLE

Have you ever felt sick to your stomach because something you worked so hard at didn't turn out as planned? Has the mere thought of failure sent you into an elevated-heart-rate, sweaty-palms, headache-type of panic attack? Have you ever been congratulated by others for reaching a goal, only to be disappointed in yourself for not doing more? If any of these hit home for you, I'm sorry to say that you are probably an overachiever.

Up until now, you might have been okay with that label. It's given you a superpower—a reputation for getting things done—that has benefitted you in life thus far. You've accomplished everything you've set out to do and then some. When people mention your name, they can't help but to also mention all of the things you've done. Having a good reputation is not a bad thing, however, when you begin to lose yourself inside of your accomplishments and live for praise, the criticism and sense of failure can be detrimental.

My fight with overachiever's syndrome dates all the way back to middle school report card day. While all my friends sat at the lunch table celebrating their passing grades, I sat panicked and crying into my arms with my head on the table. None of my friends could understand why I was so upset, and I couldn't even form the words. My friend asked to see my grades.

"My mom is going to kill me," I sobbed.

"You have all A's and B's and one C," she said, frowning.

"That C…" I said. "I'm not supposed to get C's."

My mom wasn't going to *literally* kill me, but we did have a standard in our house. A, B… fail. The reality of her reaction wasn't nearly as bad as I predicted, but that feeling never left. If I wasn't the girl who got good grades, who was I?

When your accolades begin to overshadow who you truly are as a person, you can begin to confuse the two. It is okay to have goals. Jesus' entire life was full of goals that ultimately culminated in His mission to sacrifice himself in obedience. However, your achievements should not define you to the point to where you feel lost and unidentifiable without them.

Fast forward some years, and I'm still stuck in a cycle of overachieving. However, it's different now. Something feels wrong. I've followed the plan to a tee. Go to school. Get degrees. Work hard. Remain humble. Keep working. Be compassionate. Be a good girl. Do this. Do that. *What am I even doing all of this for?* Growing up in church, I've always been told to do good and God will reward you with the desires of your heart. Well, at this point in life, I didn't have anything I desired. I wasn't working in my desired field. No husband. No kids. I was stuck on the wheel just doing things like I was supposed to, waiting for my overachieving to pay off.

"So, my dear brothers and sisters, be strong and immovable. Always work enthusiastically for the Lord, for you know that nothing you do for the Lord is ever useless" (1 Corinthians 15:58 NLT).

I had the work part DOWN! There was no doubt about it. However, was I really working in my God-given purpose; in His will for my life? There is a difference between being goal-driven in your God-given purpose and being goal-driven to people-please. Failure is okay. I know that's hard to digest, so read it again. **Failure is okay**. The only way to combat overachiever's syndrome is to reroute your brain. Why are you really doing all of these things?

God loves you so much that He gave you passions and gifts that will work for your purpose. There is no guesswork to do. All you have to do is seek Him, and it'll all fall into place. I know it doesn't seem that simple, but the lives that we plan for ourselves are just distractions. When you focus on God, the work you are supposed to do will reveal itself. The confirmation comes in little magical ways. Something so simple as a testimony from one of my editing clients can stop me in my tracks. Serving others in the literary community has been a Godsend for me to combat overachiever's syndrome. Hearing how my work has helped in some way makes me stop and say, "Okay, God...I see You." My name may not be on every best-sellers list as I dreamed of when I was younger, but being able to assist others in telling their testimonies and fulfilling their dream of becoming authors has been so much more rewarding.

When you begin to operate in your God-given purpose, you stop focusing on all you need to do and focus on all you *get* to do. It's a privilege to move with conviction. It will eliminate all the self-destructive thoughts you have because you realize it isn't about you. How amazing would it feel if you took the pressure off of yourself to be perfect? Imagine how relieved you would be if you believed that you were enough. Not what you can do for someone or what you can accomplish, but YOU. Guess what? God has already declared that you are enough. Loving Him and staying in His will is all the overachieving you need to do. Doesn't sound so bad, does it?

1 CORINTHIANS 15:58 NLT

So, my dear brothers and sisters, be strong and immovable. Always work enthusiastically for the Lord, for you know that nothing you do for the Lord is ever useless.

THOUGHTS TO CONSIDER

1. What is your biggest worry about failure?
2. Can you identify goals or aspirations in your life that are rooted in people-pleasing?

3. What are some things that you do strictly out of obligation that are not purpose driven?
4. What on your to-do list makes you feel closest to God?

A PRAYER FOR YOU

Heavenly Father,

First and foremost, I want to say thank You. Thank You for each and every gift and passion that You have placed deep within my soul. Thank You for the work that You have done through me and the lives that You have touched. Lord, I am asking for forgiveness today. Please forgive me for putting all of my gifts and talents before the Gifter. Sometimes I lose sight of who You are because of what You do through me and for that, I apologize.

Help me to not get caught up in people pleasing and to focus on providing purpose. Keep me near the cross so that I may remember that my reward is a life rooted in Your grace and not just what I do. Your Word says that as long as I stay unmovable in my faith that my work is not in vain. I thank You for showing me with Your death that I don't have to do anything to gain Your love. None of my actions can ever amount to Your sacrifice. I will continue to focus on honoring You with my gifts above all else.

In Jesus' name, I pray, amen.

ADDITIONAL SCRIPTURES ON SURRENDERING TO HIS PURPOSE

Jeremiah 29:11, Mark 14:35-36, James 4:7, 1 Peter 5:6-7, Proverbs 3:5-6, Luke 9:23, 2 Corinthians 12:9

THOUGHTS, PRAYERS, & CONVERSATIONS I NEED TO HAVE

_____

_____

_____

_____

_____

_____

_____

_____

comparison

BY AMANDA S. ANDREWS

Are you a boss? Often, when we hear the word "boss", we think of the CEO, manager, or ruler. Someone strong-willed, domineering, and making demands. However, the type of boss we should strive to be is not concerned with others' affairs. This boss is a queen who takes charge of her *own* life. A Girl B.O.S.S. is a Beautiful, Outstanding, Successful, Sister.

What makes a girl boss beautiful? Is it the style of her hair? Perhaps the makeup she wears? Maybe her beauty comes from her money, clothes, and possessions. Do those things really make us beautiful? No! A girl boss knows that her outward appearance does *not* determine her worth or define her beauty. Her beauty is found in her character. When she is patient and awaits her turn with grace, she is beautiful. Her beauty radiates when she is kind and generous to others, freely giving and sharing her resources with friends or those in need. When she gives love and respect to others, she is displaying her true beauty.

A girl boss is set apart, uniquely and wonderfully made. She stands out when others want to fit in. She sets her own pace and does not become swayed by anyone else's decisions. When her friends are heading down a path that could lead to negative consequences, she rises and takes the high road. She leads her fellow queens to victory in every situation by encouraging them to make positive choices and display regal behavior. She understands that her differences make her unique, and she is not in competition with anyone.

A girl boss is successful. She knows that success looks different for everyone. The goals we set determine our level of success, so she sets the bar high! She does not get deterred or discouraged by limitations, nor does she allow negative words to be quicksand beneath her feet. Phrases like "I can't" or "that's too hard," "I'm too young," "I'm too old," "I'm not good enough," "I'm not tall, thin, or fast enough," are *not* in her vocabulary. She only understands *I can, I will, I must, I am able, I am enough, I am worthy, I am beautiful, I am a queen.*

A girl boss is a sister to all. She knows that you can be a sister no matter what color you are, where you are from, where you grew up, what school you go to, how much money you have in the bank, or what your parents do for a living. True sisterhood is about unity. Uniting in love and strength with the queens to your right and to your left. Sisterhood is about sticking together in tough situations and standing up for one another when others try to tear you down. Sisterhood says that although we are not the same, we can celebrate our differences and find a commonality amongst us—the fact that we are all queens with big dreams.

As a girl, I was highly creative and incredibly involved in school activities. I went to college on a band scholarship and became engaged in pageantry, dance, acting, and even got voted in as the queen of my Historically Black University. After achieving many of the goals I'd set out to accomplish, my confidence reached a natural high.

Soon after, I was met with life challenges that are common among young women and girls. My carefree creativity was challenged by drama, insecurity, doubt, fear, envy, lust, low self-esteem, body image issues, and compromise. I searched for security in all the wrong places (relationships, jobs, cliques, and titles) and I set unrealistic expectations for my life based on the accomplishments of others. *She already* has a master's degree. *She is already* engaged. *She* lost so much weight. *She* started a business. *She* has *so* many followers on social media. I had so many complaints, made so many comparisons, and lost my authenticity. I believed that to *be* successful in life, I had to become like those I *thought* were successful. I had to do whatever *they* did to become recognized and accomplished.

After attempting to be someone I wasn't—dying my hair to feel pretty, buying new clothes to look skinny, having sex to feel loved, trying to emulate those around me—I learned that comparison leads to insecurity. It robs us of our destiny and extinguishes our joy. When we focus on others' accomplishments, we fail to see the beauty in our own lives. I discovered that the B.O.S.S. inside was hidden beneath my insecurities. I had to peel back the layers to reveal the truth. God has already equipped us with everything we need to be a B.O.S.S. Romans 12:5 states, "Let's just go ahead and be what we were made to be, without enviously or pridefully comparing ourselves with each other, or trying to be something we aren't" (MSG).

A girl boss does not compare herself to others. She is confident and *knows* that she is already enough. Are *you* a Girl B.O.S.S.? The answer is a resounding *yes*!

ROMANS 12:5 NLT

So it is with Christ's body. We are many parts of one body, and we all belong to each other.

THOUGHTS TO CONSIDER

1. Who have you compared yourself with lately?
2. Why do you admire them?
3. What are your strengths?
4. In what ways have you thanked God for your strengths lately?

A PRAYER FOR YOU

Lord,

You created me and You made me beautiful inside and out. Show me how to stand out when the world wants me to fit in. Help me to understand your definition of success and reach my goals. Show me how to be a sister to all who cross my path and truly walk in unity with those around me. Lord, give me the faith to believe what you said about me. You said I am beautiful, unique, forgiven, whole, and wonderfully made. You said I am the apple of your eye, I am above and not beneath, the lender and not the borrower, the head and not the tail. When I see other girls achieve great things, help me to celebrate and not try to immolate. Replace jealousy with joy and comparison with compassion. Help me to be content with what You have blessed me with and who You have called me to be. Lord, show me how to walk in confidence, live my life boldly, and live unapologetically… like a boss.

In Jesus' name, I pray, amen.

ADDITIONAL SCRIPTURES ON CONFIDENCE

Jeremiah 17:7, Galatians 1:10, Hebrews 10:35, Galatians 6:4, Philippians 6:4, Isaiah 32:17

THOUGHTS, PRAYERS, & CONVERSATIONS I NEED TO HAVE

_____

_____

_____

_____

feeling incomplete

BY LAYLA WILLIAMS

Are you in a season of feeling incomplete or unfulfilled? Or maybe you're just starting to feel a void within your heart? In my life, I remember the season when I thought I had fulfillment. I found fulfillment through my friends, family, and the Internet—but especially through my best friend. We had been best friends since second grade and we always stayed connected to one another, even when we were in different classrooms and friend groups.

We were practically sisters. We would play all the time, and I spent most of my playtime with her. We would even go over to each other's house for playdates. Without realizing it, I began to slowly believe that as long as I had her in my life, I'd be happy. In that season, I thought I had all I needed to be fulfilled, and it would last forever. Little did I know that something life-changing would happen after one of our playdates that not only changed our friendship, but changed the happiness I thought would last forever.

She and her family moved to another state after that playdate, and I had a total breakdown. I felt like a part of my heart broke and the other part of my heart was scared and alone. I cried endlessly every day after school and on the weekends, feeling the pain and emptiness in my heart growing. I didn't just cry because my best friend left; I cried wishing that the pain and emptiness would go away altogether so everything could go back to normal. I needed someone to talk to about how I felt, so I tried talking to my family. But to me, it seemed like they either didn't want to listen or thought I was being overly dramatic.

After relentlessly trying to talk to someone (or trying to bring myself to), I finally gave up. By storing all of my emotions inside, I slowly fell into a depression. I made jokes with my friends who were also struggling with depression about cutting ourselves and about what we did to make ourselves feel "happy". I didn't realize how toxic those words and feelings were to me, mentally and spiritually, which made the void and pain I felt even worse. I pretended to be happy and smile in front of others until it was natural for me. I ignored the pain because I thought others didn't care, weren't there for me, wouldn't believe I was depressed, or thought I was being a downer. Over time, the weight of holding my emotions in became overbearing—the pain was almost impossible to ignore.

There were times when I laid on my bed wondering, "What's the point of getting out of bed when there is nothing to achieve or even worth living for?" I tried filling the emptiness I felt with distractions like music, YouTube, friends—you name it. But it seemed like every puzzle piece I tried was too small to fill the huge hole within me. I remember crying in my room. I was tired of trying to fill the void because deep in my heart, I knew that I just wanted to be able to talk to someone. I wanted to talk without holding back. I wanted to spill it all.

One day, I remember clearly thinking, "Hey, God would listen." And sure enough, when I started talking to Him through prayer, I immediately began to feel the weight of my burdens lift off my heart. I could feel God coming into my heart, comforting and listening to every word I had to say. I could feel that He understood every pain I expressed and I sensed Him telling me ever so softly, "Daughter, I am here for you every single day, in every moment. I am here."

In the beginning, I didn't know who God was entirely. I just began talking to Him about the issues I was dealing with and the emotions I experienced. Then, I started wondering who God really was and wanting to know more about Him, His love, generosity, and why He showed them to me.

I started to learn more about Christianity. During that season of change and learning, God filled that void in my heart, ceased the pain, and gave me so much more than I deserved. God gave me the truth that never lies, love that never fails, and joy that never ceases. God even gave me a personal relationship with Him just for my benefit. God—a perfect person to a T—gave me—a sinful, fallen-short creation—a relationship with *Him*. On top of that, He gave me a love that was consistent, regardless of how many times I disappointed Him or committed the same mistake or sin over and over again. I have no idea where someone would find a love like that anywhere else.

Whenever I share my testimony, I recall an important verse that helps me through tough times. Romans 8:18 tells us that the pain that we feel can't compare to the joy that God will give us. God is aware of your past and present pain. He is the one who will help you through it. He will give you overwhelming joy at the end of your stormy season. God is here for you every single day waiting for you to pray to Him or surrender to Him. Say a prayer to Him right now. It doesn't matter if it's about school, that girl you want to throw hands with, something you're grateful for, or your desire to surrender your life to Him. You will never regret having a relationship with God. He is going to do amazing things in your life.

ROMANS 8:18 NLT

Yet what we suffer now is nothing compared to the glory he will reveal to us later.

THOUGHTS TO CONSIDER

1. In what ways have you felt incomplete lately?
2. Is there someone that you miss spending time with or something you miss doing?
3. What activities can you start participating in to get to know yourself better?

4. What steps can you take to get closer to God and spend time with Him more intentionally? Journaling? Painting? Exercising? Dancing?

A PRAYER FOR YOU

Heavenly Father,

Thank You for reaching out for me. Thank You for letting me be able to know Your name and have peace with You at this very moment. I pray to know You better and seek You more. I want to find fulfillment in my life through You only. I submit my life to You fully because I know that whatever You do is good. What satan has intended for evil, You have intended for good, God. Satan can no longer hold the chains he has bound to me since now I'm giving all of my worries, doubt, and sinfulness over to You.

I am no longer a slave to sin. Instead, I am a daughter of Christ. God, let these chains break today and give me a new heart in trade for this heart of stone. I invite You into my heart to begin a relationship. Help me repent while growing to be the person You want me to be in Your image. Help me clearly see Your way of living. Let me surround myself with people who bear good fruit in Your name and only Yours. Christ, all these things I pray in Your heavenly name.

Amen.

ADDITIONAL SCRIPTURES ON BELONGING

Psalm 23, Jeremiah 29:11, Revelation 3:20, 1 Peter 2:9,
John 15:19, Philippians 4:8

THOUGHTS, PRAYERS, & CONVERSATIONS I NEED TO HAVE

_____

_____

_____

_____

_____

_____

_____

_____

_____

A CONVERSATION ON...
abandonment

BY ARNETTE COLEMAN

How do you relate to others when you feel as if rejection has been embedded in your DNA? Sometimes adoption can feel like the "A" word instead of the phenomenal blessing that it truly is. The fact that you are wanted so deeply by someone can often get overshadowed by the belief that at one point, you were not wanted at all.

The adoption process itself can be long, emotional, and sometimes even costly; but in most cases, the benefits far out-weigh the burden, especially once the process is complete. Once all the I's have been dotted, the T's have been crossed, and all becomes official, there is still one more hurdle: The adoptee not only has to learn they are adopted, but now he or she must learn how to navigate the feeling of **rejection** that comes along with the knowing. The process is different for everyone, and the emotional intensity you feel is sometimes determined by how you find out. Nevertheless, once you know, you know... and thus, the struggle begins.

My journey with rejection began when I was eight years old. Someone took it upon themselves to reveal a truth about me that I did not know in the middle of a childhood disagreement—a disagreement that I do not even remember the details of! My world was rocked, to say the least! I did not believe that what I was being told was the truth, so I confronted (yes, confronted) my parents and found out that my life would never be the same again. A flood of emotions, including betrayal, shock, anger, and, yes, rejection, overpowered me at that moment. However, because I was only eight and my ninth birthday party was coming up, most of those emotions waned; my excitement for the upcoming party was the one emotion I knew how to process at the time. Not all of the emotions disappeared, though. Some settled in my heart and attempted to form my identity.

I am not sure how an eight-year-old is supposed to handle profound rejection, but I did what I thought was best for me, and I put it neatly away to continue my adolescence. It became my secret shame. There would be very few whom I would let in this shameful place. Adoption is not supposed to be shameful—after all, I had two parents that loved and provided for me as their own, but the rejection of it all still lingered in every room I entered where fathers, mothers, and children were present. Rejection lingered in family gatherings where people treated me no differently than anyone else, but it felt like I was "the one that was not like the others." Rejection lingered in conversations with friends talking about family, and it lingered particularly heavy at doctor's appointments when I had to fill out the dreaded family history form. There were times I just wanted to stand up and yell, "I DO NOT KNOW. I'M ADOPTED, OK?!" but I never did.

I had resigned myself to the fact that if my biological family did not want anything to do with me, then I did not want anything to do with them either, but curiosity got the best of me. I needed to know who I looked like and what my predispositions were, and I had to do it cautiously so I would not hurt my adoptive parents. This was, at times, a very emotional tightrope walk that often ended in disappointment. See, my adoption was not a typical one. There was no nice, neat paper trail to follow, and most of my leads turned into dead ends. As I continued my journey, there were all kinds of starts and stops, as well as emotional highs and lows, in the attempt to uncover my roots that remain out of my reach to this day.

I do not think that we are meant to start the "heavy lifting" of carrying burdens at eight years old; but that's when I started having to manage feelings and emotions before I knew what they really were. This arduous task caused me to be very shy and introverted, which did not serve me well in my teen and early young adult years. See, I was always fighting to fit in somewhere, always trying to be someone's bestie, always making sure everyone else in the room was okay while I was left wanting. Try as I did to shake that whole rejection thing, it kept creeping into my life, manifesting itself into poor decisions, indifference toward others, apathy about life, weight gain, and indulgence in adult beverages.

Alas, amid coping with an aging father in failing health, an unfinished college degree, and singleness, God saw me and He came to my rescue! He strategically placed me in the right ministry, provided the right job, and put the right people in my orbit. Once I got on this forward path, God showed me who I was in Psalm 139:13-14. He showed me that I was and am "fearfully and wonderfully made." God showed me that I am not rejected, but indeed, "accepted in the Beloved" (Ephesians 1:6). It has been a long, bumpy road. A road filled with tears, doubts, pitfalls, and delays, but also filled with "God" friends, forgiveness, and acceptance that has allowed me to embrace the truth about who God says I am.

The stigma of rejection that I had attached to adoption, which caused me so much angst through the years, has slowly dissipated. I now walk in a freedom beyond my own imagination. I have chosen forgiveness and, therefore, life! No turning back.

PSALM 139:14 NIV

I praise you because I am fearfully and wonderfully made; your works are wonderful, I know that full well.

THOUGHTS TO CONSIDER

1. Who or what has made you feel less than who God says you are?
2. Do you have the right people in your village?
3. Who do you need to forgive?

A PRAYER FOR YOU

Dear God,

Thank You so much for always coming to see about me! Even when I did not know You were watching out for me, You were there, turning obstacles into steppingstones, messes into messages, moving things and people out of the way all while putting others in place. Lord, on my very dark days when I felt most rejected and like I did not matter to anyone, You always had Your arms wide open and a listening ear ready to hear my rants and my "why me" chants. For the parents You gave, I thank You. For the path to forgiveness, I thank You. For Your loving kindness and very tender mercies, I thank You. For showing me who I am and being patient with me until I believed it, I thank You. But God, I thank You most of all for Your son, Jesus, my Savior, who fights for me daily that I might tell my story and encourage another to choose life!

In Jesus' name, amen.

ADDITIONAL SCRIPTURES ON ACCEPTANCE

Romans 8:32, Ephesians 1:15, Psalm 27:10, John 1:12, Psalm 68:5, Romans 9:26, Philippians 3:7-8

THOUGHTS, PRAYERS, & CONVERSATIONS I NEED TO HAVE

_____

_____

_____

_____

_____

_____

_____

_____

_____

_____

insignificance

BY DESIREE MICHEELS

Have you ever felt invisible? Unworthy? Utterly unspectacular? Growing up, I believed I was invisible. It wasn't like I had some superpower or magical cloak of invisibility (which actually would have been really cool). I just really didn't think people could *see* me. They looked over me, they didn't remember me, and they definitely didn't *know* me.

Because of this, I lacked confidence in my appearance and awkwardly held my shoulders up in pictures. I stood in the shadows of others whom I deemed more special, talented, or beautiful. I remained introverted in most social settings. Despite whether or not it was true, I comfortably hid behind the idea that I was invisible and rather unremarkable.

There were times where I enjoyed the spotlight. For instance, leading the church choir every Sunday or flying high in a cheer stunt at a Friday night football game. The problem was that those moments relied on what I was capable of, not *who I was*.

At church, we used to sing, "This little light of mine, I'm gonna let it shine." From a young age, I identified that "light of mine" as God and hoped people would see it. But truth be told, I was pretty sure mine was hiding under a bushel somewhere.

Now, don't get me wrong—I had a family who loved me unconditionally. They told me I was beautiful and special all the time. Still, no one had ever quite cracked through my own belief enough to change what I thought about myself. I thought that I was invisible, or better yet, not worth being seen.

That is until I turned seventeen.

Has anyone ever had one of those aha-God moments that just changed everything?

I had discovered the Jonas Brothers on Disney Channel when their song "Year 3000" came out. It was 2007, and I may have been slightly too old to like the Jonas Brothers (by society's standards), but I really didn't care what anyone thought. The Jonas Brothers had something that I wanted. They were doing something that I admired. I had to know more. I wanted to know *them*.

And so, I asked God. I said, "God, I don't know why, but I have a very strong stirring inside to know the Jonas Brothers personally… and I want them to know me, too. I want them to remember me. Do with that what you will."

That July, my best friend and I got to see the Jonas Brothers in concert for the first time. We even got to meet them after the show. So, as you can imagine, my yearning to know them only grew stronger. I had written them a letter telling them how much their songs meant to me. In it, I shared that I was a musician, too, and that I was so grateful for their example.

The summer went on, and I went to a few more concerts. Three weeks after I met them for the first time, I received an email from one of the three brothers. I—invisible Desirée, the wallflower who never made a ruffle or a lasting impression—got an email from one of the people I desired to know most.

Small break for a freak out here! Did this Jonas Brother seriously meet me, along with a million other girls, read my letter, and take a moment out of his crazy Jonas Brother schedule to email *me* and ask *me* for my phone number? This has to be some kind of mistake... I'm invisible!

Except it wasn't a mistake. It was God. It was God answering my ridiculously harebrained request (from just a few weeks earlier) to know the Jonas Brothers and to be remembered by them. It was God saying, "I SEE YOU, DESIREE." And more than that, "*I know* you," and "You are beautiful to ME."

Ladies, I'm just going to give you a moment to step into this seventeen-year-old-dream-come-true; this moment of transformation where God held up a mirror and showed me myself through *His* eyes for the first time. In His most personal and intimate nature, He met me where I was to reveal a truth I'd never known or believed: I wasn't invisible. I wasn't invisible to the people around me, to the Jonas Brother who I watched on TV, or most importantly, to God.

Through that answered prayer, I learned that God not only saw me, but that He knew my heart's deepest desires. I wasn't just noticed; I was *known*.

Despite what I may have believed about myself or what I thought I saw when I looked in the mirror, the truth was that the

God of the universe designed and defined me. He traded my cloak of invisibility for a crown of confidence. His love validated, empowered, purposed, and pursued me—a revelation that enlightened the eyes of my heart to what He called me to, as we read in Ephesians 1:18.

I can only imagine that if God heard my somewhat ridiculous seventeen-year-old request, He definitely hears your desires, too. He knows your heart even better than you do. So, seek Him. Ask Him. Trust Him. Stop wondering, "why me?" and start asking, "why *not* me?" You are *not* invisible. You are a beautiful daughter of the Most High King, and He wants to give you the desires of your heart (Psalm 37:4).

EPHESIANS 1:18-19 NIV

I keep asking that the God of our Lord Jesus Christ, the glorious Father, may give you the Spirit of wisdom and revelation, so that you may know him better. I pray that the eyes of your heart may be enlightened in order that you may know the hope to which he has called you, the riches of his glorious inheritance in his holy people, and his incomparably great power for us who believe.

THOUGHTS TO CONSIDER

1. Who or what has defined what you believe about your identity and self-worth?
2. How has God designed you to stand apart?
3. Is there something on your heart that you would boldly entrust God with? What is it and have you given it to Him?

A PRAYER FOR YOU

Father God,

Divine Designer of the heavens and earth, I am so humbled to know that amongst Your most incredible and miraculous creations, You made me. You called me Yours and chose me to be a light for Your Kingdom. Before I was born, You knew me, Lord. You counted the hairs on my head and the steps on my path. I am comforted and uplifted to know that I am seen and known by You, Lord God. Father, I pray that I would always have a Spirit of wisdom and revelation to know what You are calling me to, to know my divine inheritance as a daughter of the King, and to rest and rely in Your infinite power. Thank You, Father, for pursuing my life, for purposing me, and for preparing me for what You have in store.

In Jesus' mighty name, I thank You, I praise You.

ADDITIONAL SCRIPTURES ON BEING SEEN BY GOD

Genesis 16:13, 1 Samuel 16:7, Psalm 33:18, Psalm 139, 1 John 5:14, Jeremiah 29:12-13

THOUGHTS, PRAYERS, & CONVERSATIONS I NEED TO HAVE

idealism

BY CHRISTINE PRATO-COLEMAN

Can you remember a time when you believed in fairytales? Growing up, I surely did. I believed in dreams coming true. I believed in the Disney beginning—"Once upon a time"—and the happily ever after ending.

I'd imagined and romanticized how God wanted this for us—how His original intent was that we live a life that was beautiful and perfect.

It was around age four that my mother introduced me to her favorite fairytale, Cinderella. It quickly became my favorite, too. I fell in love with Cinderella and her story. I admired how kind she was and I loved her song. "No matter how your heart is grieving, if you keep on believing, the dream that you wish will come true."

I was certain we could experience a fairytale life if we believed deeply enough—like Cinderella—and I did... to the very core of my being. Holding on to that belief my entire life, I eventually wrote a book entitled *Just Believe*. How's that for a testimony?

Due to my convictions, every time I experienced adversity, I was shocked and disappointed. People insisted I take off the rose-colored glasses. I'd constantly hear, "Face reality, Christine! Life is *not* a Disney movie!"

I refused to allow cynics to dictate my hopefulness or my sunny outlook. Call me naïve, but I held a high set of ideals. But what does *ideal* mean anyway? It means satisfying one's conception of what is perfect, existing **only** in the imagination, desirable, but not likely to become a reality. WHAT? I chose not to believe that my ideals couldn't be realized. Instead, I pressed on. I lived by my ideals and shared them with likeminded people. I raised a daughter who would follow in her mother's footsteps, just like I did.

So, what was it about Cinderella that we admired so much? What captivated us about her and her story? Was it the supernatural appearance of her Fairy Godmother whose powers transformed mice into gallant horses or an ordinary pumpkin into a dazzling stagecoach? Perhaps it was the sprinkling of stardust that magically refashioned her rags into a stunning ballgown? Or was it that something so wonderful happened for such an unlikely young lady?

When someone stays hopeful in dreadful circumstances and does the right thing—even when the right thing isn't happening for them—it more than tugs at your heartstrings; it inspires you to do the same.

It wasn't until my seventeen-year-old daughter—another unlikely young lady—received an answer to her outrageous prayer, that God validated my crazy belief that fairytales do come true. And though the experience we shared was quite the rollercoaster ride, my daughter and I grew stronger in our faith than ever before. We relished in the abundance of God's unmerited favor and gave Him the glory for the supernatural circumstances He allowed. It was almost too good to be true. As the skeptics in our lives waited for the other shoe to drop (a little Cinderella humor), we relied on God's guidance, the promises *He* made, and *His* provision.

One day, without warning, the plug was pulled on our fairytale. The rollercoaster ride came to an end. The happily ever after we envisioned fell to pieces. This was a pivotal moment for me. Was I going to replace my life's principles with pessimism? Give in to the naysayers? I knew God could work any circumstance for our good, but struggled to see a way through this particular heartache.

Then, it hit me: We didn't fall in love with Cinderella's story because she was beautiful and married the Prince. We fell in love with her because *she overcame hardship, stayed beautiful, and her faithfulness was rewarded.*

That was an aha moment for me... rewarded for being faithful.

You see, the ball Cinderella attended was thrown by the King to prompt his son, Prince Charming, to find a bride. She was not only an unlikely attendee, but an improbable match for the Prince. While she delighted in the favor of dancing in his arms, she knew everything would return to the way it was when midnight struck: rags for clothes, stagecoach to pumpkin, horses to mice. She dashed at the sound of the clock's chime, dropping her shoe as she ran back to the cinders of her life.

Unbeknownst to Cinderella, after fleeing the gala, Prince Charming declared his love for her. And the King, knowing the Prince's heart, sent forth the Grand Duke to search the entire kingdom for her. With only a glass slipper to identify her, they set out on a relentless search until Cinderella was found. She would become the Prince's bride. There would be an exchange... a crown of beauty for ashes.

Isn't that just what God the Father did for us? Didn't He send His Son, Jesus, the Bridegroom, to redeem us from eternal cinders? Didn't He pursue us by leaving the ninety-nine to find the one? Doesn't He offer us beauty for ashes?

Yes. The love story is that *He* is faithful. The divine exchange He offers us is a crown of beauty instead of ashes, the oil of gladness instead of mourning, and a garment of praise instead of a spirit of despair.

Though our fairytale experience did not have the classic Disney ending, it gave way to more blessings than we could count. James 1:12 reminds us, "Blessed is the one who perseveres under trial because having stood the test, they will receive the crown of life that the Lord has promised to those who love Him." It was that scripture that prompted me to offer the sacrifice of praise. And though praise may not have been on the top of my to-do list after our heartache, the decision to heed God's Word was.

While our faithfulness is rewarded, our hope in *His* faithfulness—when He comes for His bride, the church—is the happily-ever-after ending we eagerly await.

ISAIAH 61:3 NIV

Bestow on them a crown of beauty instead of ashes, the oil of joy instead of mourning, and a garment of praise instead of a spirit of despair.

THOUGHTS TO CONSIDER

1. In what ways do perfectionism and/or idealism shape your actions and beliefs?
2. Do you handle hardship with grace or grumbling? How can you be an example for others to remain hopeful amidst adversity?
3. What ashes do you need to let go of to receive the crown of beauty that God promises?

A PRAYER FOR YOU

Dear Lord,

I am so grateful to You, Father, for Your faithfulness. I know Your original plan for us was to live a perfect life, and though I struggle with my human nature to try to make everything in this life perfect, I know You alone are flawless. I thank You for the sacrificial gift of Your Son, Jesus, who offers me a crown of beauty for ashes, who loves me with all of my imperfections and shortcomings. Help me to see that through hardship and trials, You are preparing ordinary me for an extraordinary destiny. I submit to You, Lord, and hand over all that I am for all that You are.

In Jesus' name, it is Your everlasting joy that I seek. Amen.

ADDITIONAL SCRIPTURES ON THE PERFECTION OF GOD

Psalm 84:10, Hebrews 10:23, Habakkuk 2:3, Romans 8:28, Colossians 3:1-2, Revelation 1:17

THOUGHTS, PRAYERS, & CONVERSATIONS I NEED TO HAVE

_____

_____

_____

_____

_____

_____

_____

anxiety

BY SHALESE JOHNSON

Have you ever woken up in the middle of the night—panicked, heart racing, unable to go back to sleep? Have you ever had the feeling like something terrible was bound to happen, but you had no control over it? On the outside, things may have looked perfectly fine, but internally, you were a mess.

Recently, I experienced this every night for months, but it didn't end there. I was battling anxiety. I battled it throughout the day, and it made me feel like I had no control over my body or my mind. Even when I tried to change my thinking, my body responded with worry and fear. My battle with anxiety was rough. However, I was glad to know that I was not fighting this battle alone. I was glad to know that there was, and is, a source that will set me free from anxiety. This source is eternal and it will never run dry. It's simply... *JESUS.* In the midst of it all, I was fortified—*secured*—in Christ. Through His Word and worship, I received victory in Christ Jesus over the enemy. If you've ever struggled with anxiety, I want you to know you can have victory, too.

A few months ago, I found myself in the bathroom, cold and shaking. It was early in the early morning. I called to my mother to come and be near me. My heart rate was so high. I had awaken in a panic. These frightening feelings were coming more frequently. Just weeks before that, I found myself leaning on the front door, head in my arms, breathing slowly and taking in the fresh air. I called to my brother to have someone near at that time, as well, because my heart rate was, again, so high. Each panic attack came on suddenly and shook me to my core. It seemed as though my heart was going to beat right out of my chest. I needed to rest, but I was afraid to go to sleep. How did I get through it? I was reminded that there was someone Whom I could call on Who would see me through it all. I literally overcame this by calling on the name of Jesus in prayer and worship, and by applying His Word.

These panic attacks were sporadic. They came at times where I was overwhelmed, worried, and nervous. I decided to look to God to better understand and identify the triggers of these attacks. I researched and read about the symptoms that I was having. We know the enemy walks around seeking whom he can devour, but I also asked God to expose *my* part in it because He knows me better than I know myself. I had to know if there was anything I was doing or neglecting to do to contribute to what I was experiencing. Was God trying to get my attention? I needed God to help me. He wanted me to seek Him.

In Philippians 4:6-7, God's Word reminds us to not be anxious for anything, but to come to God in prayer for everything. Sis, nothing is too little or too big for God. We are reminded to come with thanksgiving and let our requests be made known to Him, so I decided to pray my way through those panic attacks. I worshipped my way through the anxiety and proclaimed the Word of God over my life. I asked God to renew my mind every moment of the day. When I did, I was able to get closer to God, and He began to reveal to me what my triggers were. I was able to use wisdom to take actionable steps to overcome them, and they no longer overcame me. I continued to pray to God and call those things out by name, allowing Him to remove and uproot them from my life. Praise and worship filled my space at night and it drowned out the lies of the enemy and the loud thumps of my heart. It allowed me to fall into the arms of Jesus. As He carried me through the night, I slept peacefully in His presence.

Over time, the attacks became less frequent, and the anxiety less effective. No one was mad but the devil. Whenever I spoke God's name or spoke His Word, my heart rate would begin to lower. My life was returning to normal, and, most importantly, I was able to have peace. At the end of verse 7 in Philippians 6, there's a promise that if we do all these things, the peace of God, which surpasses all understanding, will guard our hearts and minds through Christ Jesus. The promise that God's supernatural peace will guard our hearts and minds is profound! Yes, please! This peace is not based on circumstances, but on Christ, our Lord. God used this process to strengthen me in Christ, and, today, the access points the enemy once used are no longer readily available to him.

So, how are we able to win the battle and have victory over anxiety? We do this by seeking God and fortifying ourselves in Him. We seek Him through prayer and choosing to quiet down to hear Him reply. God's Word, the Bible, is the Sword of the Spirit. His Word is alive and sharper than any double-edged sword. Reading, applying, and meditating on His Word day and night is key. Remember, worship is a weapon! It's a weapon we have to lift up in the name of Jesus to overcome the enemy and shift things in the spiritual realm. Those things we think and speak are either giving life or death to situations that we face. Most importantly, our trust, faith, and hope must be in the Lord. When we do so, we are able to deliver a mighty defeat to the tricks and plans of the enemy. We are able to enjoy the freedom and the peace that supersedes our situations and even our own understanding.

PHILIPPIANS 4:6-7 NIV

Do not be anxious about anything, but in every situation, by prayer and petition, with thanksgiving, present your requests to God. And the peace of God, which transcends all understanding, will guard your hearts and your minds in Christ Jesus.

THOUGHTS TO CONSIDER

1. What are some triggers that you believe God has shown you that the enemy is using as an access point to your mind and spirit when it comes to anxiety?
2. Are there any areas in your life where you are overcommitted or overwhelmed? How can those be valued with God so that you are not taking on what's not in God's will for your life?
3. Write out some ways you can grow spiritually and be safer or **fortified** in Christ.

A PRAYER FOR YOU

Father God,

I come to You thanking You for who You are. I thank You, Lord, for Your heart and Your unconditional mercy, grace, and love that You bestow on me daily. Thank You for breathing life into me today and allowing me to further serve You, glorify You, and advance Your Kingdom. I confess of my sins and repent of my sins. I ask for Your forgiveness of my sins. Jesus, I need You. My mind and spirit is uneasy, restless, and worried. I know in You that I don't have to worry or fret. Help me to seek Your face, God, and Your kingdom. I bind up anxiety in the name of Jesus from my life and my bloodline right now. I release peace, God, in Your name. I bind up and rebuke the enemy and cast him to the pits of hell. I pray for a supernatural level of peace in my home, my mind, my heart, and in my spirit, God. I ask that that You expose me to me and help me walk according to Your will and purpose for my life. Let me hear Your voice. Let me have a peaceful day, restful night, and worry no more.

In Jesus' name I pray, amen.

ADDITIONAL SCRIPTURES ON PEACE

Psalm 46:10, Isaiah 26:3, Psalm 34:4, Exodus 14:14, John 14:27, John 16:33

THOUGHTS, PRAYERS, & CONVERSATIONS I NEED TO HAVE

_____

_____

_____

_____

_____

_____

fear

BY DENISE LANE

Have you ever cried yourself to sleep or stayed up all night with knots in your stomach? Fear can cause all kinds of reactions. Fear can make you physically ill. It can cause panic attacks and it can force you to make the wrong decision. How do you fight fear? I fight fear with faith.

Growing up, I had a great childhood. I never wanted much. I was raised in a two-parent household and I grew up in charming neighborhoods. My dad was a great provider, and my mom was an entrepreneur. We always had our own home. I had a grandmother who spoiled me crazy. I went to Sunday school, sang in the choir, and went to church regularly. I got good grades in school and went to a good college. In 1970, when my parents took me to Spelman's campus, helped me unpack, and then departed, I was afraid. It was my first time away from home and I didn't know anyone, but I learned how to fight my fear with faith. According to Hebrews 11:1, "Faith is confidence in what we hope for and assurance about what we do not see."

After college, I went back to New Jersey and began a career as an administrator in the nonprofit world. Life was good. All of my friends were married and had started their families, so I was thankful when I found someone I thought would be a good husband and father. In 1980, when my father walked me down the aisle and asked me if I was sure I wanted to get married, I was afraid. I didn't know if I would be a good wife or a good mother, but I learned to fight my fears with faith.

We got married, and it was six years before I had my son. In 1985, when the doctors found a lump in my left breast and had to perform a lumpectomy—even though I was four months pregnant—I was afraid. What if something was really wrong and it affected my pregnancy? Instead of worrying, I chose to fight my fears with faith. Five months later, when I was sick during my pregnancy, the doctor would not let me leave the office because he wanted me to be transported to the hospital for an emergency C-section. I was afraid, but I put my trust in God and fought my fears with faith.

The demands of work, mothering, and being involved in the community presented a challenge, but I rose to it. Two years later, I became pregnant with my daughter, and that's when I realized I was doing it all by myself. My husband had other interests, which left the kids and me to make it on our own. When he started drinking excessively and threatened my life, I knew it was time to make a move. For our own well-being, I thought it best to move to Las Vegas. My mother lived there. The kids had spent holidays and some of the summer break with her, so it seemed natural to go there. In 1996, when I packed up my two children and our belongings to drive from New Jersey to Las Vegas to start a new life, I was terrified. I was afraid of what I might meet on the way; I was afraid of what kind of house I had rented, sight unseen; I was afraid of not being able to find a job to take care of my family; I was afraid of being alone without my friends; I was afraid of how my children would react to entirely new surroundings. I remember the fear all too well, but I made it through. I fought my fears with faith.

For a long time, I thought my husband would come to Las Vegas to be with his family. I hated that the children did not have their dad, but he never came to stay or take us back to New Jersey, so we made Las Vegas our home. We found a good solid church. I found a job, got the kids enrolled in school, and began studying the Word. This was when I realized how important it is to have a relationship with Jesus. I fought my fears with my faith and realized God had been answering my prayers all along.

In every instance, I called upon God to help me. He may not have answered me immediately, but he answered. I know it was because of my faith. I may not have understood the power of prayer or faith long ago, however, I always remembered that my Nana told me to call upon Jesus in times of fear. Once you know Jesus and believe in His Word, you will understand that having faith can calm all fears. It was faith that brought me through the hard times, and it is faith that keeps me going day today.

My children are grown now and have their own families, As I watch my tweenage granddaughters grow up in this crazy world, I realize that I'm afraid again. I look at my granddaughters and I fear the unknown, their safety, and futures. I see some of the poor choices they make and pray that God will keep them safe. I'm afraid because like many young ladies today, some of their decisions are questionable. I'm afraid because their circles of friends are sometimes undesirable. I'm afraid because the Internet and social media give them too much information that may be inappropriate for their age. I'm afraid for their lives when they go to and from school. I have so many fears. I have spent so many nights crying, but I continue to pray to God and have faith that He will answer my prayers and keep them safe.

Now that I understand the true meaning of faith, I want my children and grandchildren to learn about God's greatness. Should they face a difficult situation, I want them to remember this scripture. "'For I know the plans I have for you,' declares the Lord, 'plans to prosper you and not to harm you, plans to give you hope and a future'" (Jeremiah 29:11). I want them to know who God is because I know that building a relationship with God will help them find their purpose and strengthen their faith. I want them to know that they are beautiful without all the makeup and revealing clothes. I want them to know that social media can sometimes be harmful and that their parents know what is best for them at their ages. I want them to know that having a phone or a boyfriend is not the most important thing in the world, even though it can feel like it. I want them to know that God always has a plan for us, and it's not to hurt us but to give us hope and a future. I want them to know that they can always call on the Lord in times of need. Because of faith, Peter walked on water, Moses parted the Red Sea, Noah built the Ark. Because of Jesus, I was able to move to Las Vegas, raise my children as a single mom, and provide for them.

Because I fight fear with faith, I know in my heart that my granddaughters will grow up to be outstanding, successful young women. I know that God will watch over them and keep them safe from harm. I have faith that they will look back and remember how I kept them covered with the love of Jesus while growing up. I have faith that whenever they have fear, they will remember how I showed them to fight fear with faith. God is the author of scripture, and I put my trust in him. You can put your trust in him too. Just fight the fear with faith.

HEBREWS 11:1 NIV

Now faith is confidence in what we hope for and assurance about what we do not see.

THOUGHTS TO CONSIDER

1. What encouragement have you received in times of fear?

2. What scriptures come to mind when you are fearful?

3. What does faith mean to you?

4. How can you strengthen your faith?

A PRAYER FOR YOU

Father God,

     Please hear my prayer. Bless Your holy name, Jesus. I love You, Lord, and I thank You for every day You wake me. I thank You for the air I breathe, the food I eat, and the roof over my head. I thank You for the opportunity to have conversations with You. I thank You for coming into my life and washing away my fears and strengthening my faith. Thank You for loving me. I thank You Lord for all the blessings You have bestowed on me. Thank You for the people in my life and allowing me to be a positive role model in their lives. Thank You, Lord, for forgiving my sins. I rebuke the spirit of fear, anxiety, and other negative feelings in the name of Jesus. I put my faith and trust in Your holy words. I thank You, Lord, for always being there for me, in good times and bad. Thank You for never leaving me. Thank You for the ability to fight my fears with faith. I thank You for the opportunity to share my story with others in hopes that they will know the works of the Lord. I pray that others will learn that God is King and that the Kingdom of God is available to everyone.

     In the name of Jesus I pray, amen.

ADDITIONAL SCRIPTURES ON FAITH

Joshua 1:9, Psalm 56:4, Isaiah 41:10, Hebrews 11:1,
Philippians 4:19, Romans 8:15, 1 John 4:4

THOUGHTS, PRAYERS, & CONVERSATIONS
I NEED TO HAVE

_____

_____

_____

_____

_____

_____

_____

_____

_____

unforgiveness

BY NATASHA LAU-JOHNSON

Have you ever made a decision that you thought would not be forgiven by God?

At the premature age of seventeen years old, I became a teenage mother. In a blink of an eye, in a moment of flesh and emotion, I made a decision that changed the course of my entire life. Unprepared and scared, I learned quickly that this life—my life—was not about me. I was raised in a military household, often traveling from city to city. My parents decided to settle our family in Las Vegas, Nevada, and I met the father of my child at the very young age of twelve. I was misguided, uncertain, and looking for love and acceptance from a relationship. It was my first real relationship, and all my thoughts and decisions were led by my emotions. I knew who God was. I was raised in a household that taught me respect; a household that reinforced the importance of manners; a household grounded in love. Still,

I found myself making decisions about my life, body, and relationships that were not grounded in the respect I'd learned for my body, the value I was expected to place in my future, or the honor I felt toward God.

I remember my first sexual experience and how shameful I felt. In the midst of that shame, I continued to sacrifice my value and my worth in sexual sin. I vividly remember feeling like I was living a double life. While I was respectful to others, followed the rules, and maintained good grades, I felt dishonest with myself. There was a part of me that needed to be validated in a relationship. That need for validation resulted in a lack of regard for my body and my life.

My pregnancy was the first domino that led to many more bad decisions that I would make in my teen and young adult years. Those decisions were made from a place within me that neglected to believe I was worthy, valued, or respected. Today, I can see how raising my daughter at such a young age has affected her life in ways that I continuously pray about. She grew up in two different households and, at an early age, was required to, essentially, live in two different worlds. Although I didn't understand it when I was seventeen, I truly understand the importance of not having sex before marriage now. It has so many negative effects, like having to raise children in a broken family. Today, I recognize that my daughter represents God's grace and unconditional love in my life, and I'm so grateful for His continued presence.

As I reflect on my journey as a teenage mother, I think about God's Word in Isaiah 61:3 which states that God will "Bestow on them a crown of beauty instead of ashes, the oil of joy instead of mourning, and a garment of praise instead of a spirit of despair." In the Bible, it was the custom for people to cover themselves with ashes to express grief over a distressful situation or the grief they felt when repenting sin.

Today, I can clearly see that God turned the ashes of my sexual sin, the lack of honor for my body, and the decisions I made without seeking Him in prayer into a crown of beauty. I can see the beauty in my daughter, who committed to her own relationship with God well before I did. I can see the beauty in the purpose God has placed upon my life to minister to young ladies about their personal relationship with God. I can see the beauty in the opportunity I have to share how the intimate relationship we have with the Heavenly Father can guide all other relationships. In the midst of the ashes, God is mercy, forgiveness, grace, and unconditional love. I encourage you to know God—to really know Him on an intimate level. Let your relationship with God be the example for the current and future relationships that you will have along life's journey.

If I could go back and give my younger self advice, I would tell her that honoring your body today is your choice to honor your future for tomorrow. I would remind her that there is so much life ahead of her and that she will one day find the right person to begin a family with. I would speak to her lovingly and gracefully as I pour words of encouragement, accountability, and wisdom into her life because I know where she is. I would remind her that her life journey begins now and encourage her to begin living a life pleasing to God's sight and honoring to God's Word. I would also tell her that she will make mistakes along her way, but that those mistakes will help define the person she will become. God will give her a crown of beauty in exchange for her ashes.

When I look at my life today, I can see that God turned my ashes to beauty for His glory. The amazing thing about God and His grace is that in our darkest moments, when we think that we can never be forgiven for our mistakes, He never leaves or forsakes us. Remember that God created us—every hair on our head. He created our personality, our intellect, and our will. He knows our every thought and every choice we will make before we make it. Knowing that, I encourage you to choose God, to choose His Word, to choose His Grace, and to choose His Love. Allow God to turn your ashes to beauty and wear your crown boldly!

ISAIAH 61:3 NIV

And provide for those who grieve in Zion—to bestow on them a crown of beauty instead of ashes, the oil of joy instead of mourning, and a garment of praise instead of a spirit of despair. They will be called oaks of righteousness, a planting of the Lord for the display of his splendor.

THOUGHTS TO CONSIDER

1. Can you remember a time that you made a decision in a relationship that did not honor self-respect for your body?
2. Have you ever felt as though you had to lower your standards in order to fit in or feel accepted by another person?
3. How does Isaiah 61:3 relate to your life?
4. What are the "ashes" in your life that you want God to turn into your crown of beauty?

A PRAYER FOR YOU

Heavenly Father,

Thank You for Your mercy and unconditional love for me. I may not always make the right decisions, but I want to honor You. So right now, I ask for Your Word to be the light along my path. I surrender my body, my mind, my thoughts, and my emotions to You, because I know that You will care for them, hold them, and allow them to be honoring to You. I humbly ask for Your forgiveness for the moments in my life that I did not seek You first—before entering in that relationship, for not setting boundaries for my body, thoughts, and emotions, and for not remembering that my body is a temple that I should treat as royalty. Today, I commit my everything to You. I desire to know You and to follow Your Word. Heavenly Father, have Your way in my life, as I continue to seek You first, in all ways and all things.

In Your holy name, amen.

ADDITIONAL SCRIPTURES ON FORGIVENESS

Lamentations 3:22-23, John 3:16, Romans 5:8, Romans 8:1, Romans 8:35-39, 2 Corinthians 5:17, Matthew 6:14, 1 John 1:9

THOUGHTS, PRAYERS, & CONVERSATIONS I NEED TO HAVE

_____

_____

_____

_____

_____

_____

_____

_____

_____

_____

rejection

BY JACQUELINE HARRIS-SMITH

How did you feel the first time you experienced rejection? Pain? Disgusting? Unwanted? Angry? Rejection is a word that in and of itself conjures up negative thoughts and sometimes, negative feelings. Rejection—or the act feeling rejected—is not an experience we desire. We never want to feel rejected because it can feel gross or disgusting, and it makes us feel less than the person who denied us in the first place.

Plenty of people can relate to the pain, hurt, or disappointment of being the child who was among the last to get picked at recess to play the latest playground game. Those incidents implanted an early social stigma of rejection. However, most of the time, we were able to go home and relay the day's events to our parents without feeling worse. Thankfully, for many of us, our parents wisely imparted loving words of encouragement, affirmation, and the boost of confidence that was necessary for our self-esteem.

My question is: What do you do when you feel as if rejection is present in your home, too? Rejection that is just a figment of your imagination feels just as real. Can we talk about that a little? I'd like to share some of my story with you.

One of the coolest things about growing up in a two-parent household with parents who came together in marriage from different states is that you often get to travel to visit extended family. My dad is from Texas, and my mom is from South Carolina; so when we visited family, it was via road trip from New Jersey, where I was born and raised, to South Carolina, and then on to Texas. Now, given my age, this was back when there were no cell phones, handheld games, or anything other than your imagination to entertain you in the car. Books and music (cassette tapes anyone?) could engage your mind for a while, but those road trips gave me plenty of time to think about what happened on our vacation. One of those trips to Texas stands out vividly in my memory to this day.

The experience that I interpreted as rejection happened as soon as my family walked into my aunt's home to visit. I was about ten years old. I walked in the house in front of my sister, but, for some reason, my aunt didn't seem to acknowledge me. She just acknowledged my sister. That may seem small or insignificant, but it stayed on my mind and captivated my attention for the rest of the trip. I kept obsessing over why she hadn't complimented me in the same way when I walked through the door. I don't think there was any malicious intent, but her choice to withhold the compliment from me made me feel like I didn't fit into my father's side of the family.

I have to admit that what I didn't know at the time was that my dad—the one and only man I have ever known as my father—is not actually my biological father. My young spirit still picked up and adopted the sense of rejection I felt in the moment, though. Little did I know, it would soon grow into a longing to be accepted and to meet the approval of everyone.

I didn't like being overlooked. I certainly didn't want to feel like I had done anything to push someone away, so I decided to become the girl that everyone liked. Unfortunately, that set off a silent war within my spirit and my soul for a long time. Looking back on it, I guess I just wanted to be someone's girl— so I became the girl from around the way that all the guys liked. I even used to say that I got along better with boys than girls, not realizing that I was feeding myself a lie from the enemy.

U4 is an algebraic base formula, and I think that it provides a really good analogy for the trap the evil one attempts to create for us. The devil wants to keep us feeling Unloved, Unworthy, Unaccepted, and Under his control. However, our algebraic answer to his U4 rejection formula is Romans 8:38-39, which reads, "And I am convinced that nothing can ever separate us from God's love. Neither death nor life, neither angels nor demons, neither our fears for today nor our worries about tomorrow—not even the powers of hell can separate us from God's love. No power in the sky above or in the earth below— indeed, nothing in all creation will ever be able to separate us from the love of God that is revealed in Christ Jesus our Lord," in the New Living Translation.

If I had an open line of communication with my mom, I might have been able to go to her with my issues from the beginning. Problem is, that was not the type of relationship we had; so my issues morphed into risky, promiscuous behaviors. The girl from around the way—me—would hide behind the gym with guys. She would cut school to hang out at the neighborhood boy's house with several of his friends. She would accept the actions of domestic violence against her, all in an effort to appease them.

Since I had built my identity on the lie that I had to make people like me, this behavior continued throughout my teen years and followed me into my early military career. My way of thinking was that for a guy to like me, I had to give in to his physical desires. But it was never as simple as that. Feelings of guilt and shame overpowered my sense of self-worth and led me to develop a non-confrontational personality so that I could maintain any relationship in my life.

Thankfully, I had a conversation with a mature Christian woman who knocked on my front door one day. I asked her, "How do you really know that God loves you?" I don't remember the entirety of the conversation, but what I do remember is the sincerity in which she shared Jesus' love for me. In her loving patience, she proceeded to tell me of God's endless, unconditional love for me that covered me no matter what I had done in the past.

That conversation changed the trajectory of my relationships. I began a journey that led from simply knowing of God to pursuing an intimate relationship with Him. I am still on this journey becoming who God has called me to be in Him.

I don't consider myself to have reached my full potential. What I do know is that as an encourager, I am called to encourage, uplift, and let my sisters know that they are fully loved, adored, and favored by God. Regardless of what has happened in your past, you can move forward in His strength because of His unfailing love for you. Mothers, mentors, aunties, and gramtees—talk to your daughters and mentees to let them know that rejection is a part of life, but we can navigate through it together.

ROMANS 8:38-39 NIV

For I am convinced that neither death nor life, neither angels nor demons, neither the present nor the future, nor any powers, neither height nor depth, nor anything else in all creation, will be able to separate us from the love of God that is in Christ Jesus our Lord.

THOUGHTS TO CONSIDER

1. What may be causing you to feel rejection in your circle of friends and how do you deal with that rejection?
2. Have you ever felt as if God has rejected you?

3. Read Joshua 1:9. In what ways could you apply this verse to an instance where you may face rejection?

A PRAYER FOR YOU

Father,

I am so very grateful that I am a chosen daughter, handpicked by You. I am thankful that in You, there is no rejection, fear, or longing to belong. I am Yours and You are mine, so please help me to always remember that. I thank You for the reassurance that You love me with a love that runs so very deep that I cannot even begin to imagine the very depths of just how deeply You love me. Thank You for telling me that I am the apple of Your eye, that I am fearfully and wonderfully made, and Your works are wonderful.

I long to have an intimate relationship with You that never grows stale and always keeps me rooted and grounded in You. I ask that You allow me to remember to declare my allegiance to You daily. Day by day, be my suitable helper to guide me along life's path as the Holy Spirit illuminates the way. I pray that You cover me and be the lifter of my head when I start to doubt myself and Your will for my life. Father, forgive me for ever doubting Your love for me. Please forgive me for not trusting You with the cares and concerns of my heart. As I open up to You, speak to my heart in the way that reaches me so that all doubt is erased from me and does not cause any interference. Thank You for my life and loving me through it all.

In the matchless name of Jesus I pray, amen.

ADDITIONAL SCRIPTURES ON SECURITY

Psalm 139:17-18, 1 Peter 2:4, Romans 8:31, Luke 6:22-23, Proverbs 21:21, 1 Corinthians 13:4-5

THOUGHTS, PRAYERS, & CONVERSATIONS I NEED TO HAVE

_____

_____

_____

_____

_____

_____

_____

_____

abuse

BY ROBIN TURNER

When you hear that our God has not given us a spirit of fear, what is the first question that comes to mind? The first question I have is: then why do people experience fear? You can ask anyone and, if they are honest, they will tell you that they have experienced fear in some capacity.

I want to talk about fear, doubt, and insecurity. But let's take it one step further—let's talk about how we can overcome it all. My story begins when I was eight years old. My mother worked a graveyard shift at the hospital and she often needed to leave me in the care of someone during the week. She chose to leave me at her uncle's house. She had a friendly relationship with his wife, so she trusted her to watch me and keep a close eye on me. Since I would be dropped off at their house really late at night, I often had to sleep in the bed with one of my cousins, who were much older than I was.

I often slept in the bed with my cousin whom I will call "Taylor." Taylor was around twenty-one years old, but she could have been older. When she was not at home, she hated for anyone to be in her room. That meant I had to sleep in the room with the boys who were around the ages of sixteen and seventeen. I was often told to get in the bed with my cousin, whom I will call "Marvin." Marvin was the last person I thought would have touched me inappropriately, but he did. It started with him touching me inappropriately, but it didn't stop there. It escalated into him choosing to do things with an eight-year-old girl that no one ever should.

Marvin touched me on more than one occasion, and I believe that this was when I learned to hide my truth. I did not tell anyone initially. Fear made me keep quiet. The fear of hurting my mom—and the fear of her losing her close friend whom she had entrusted to watch me—bound my mouth shut. I felt so much shame and guilt. Even though it wasn't my fault, since he was older and knew better, I couldn't shake the guilt. I carried the shame and the guilt with me every day, and I decided to bury it and act as though it had not happened.

When I was around eleven or twelve years old, it changed. As my mother was getting ready for work, she instructed me to get ready so that she could drop me off at my uncle's house again. I felt courageous and bold that particular day, so I told my mother, "I do not want to go over their house."

When my mother asked me why, I remember simply stating, "I just don't want to go."

My mother asked, "So you are going to stay in this house by yourself?"

I thought about it carefully because, I will be honest, I was afraid of being home alone. We didn't live in the best area. I decided being at home was much better than being at their house and going through the abuse again, so I simply said, "Yes." The choice to stay home ended that particular cycle of abuse for me, but there was a deeply rooted fear that anyone would learn my secret; it stayed with me long after I stopped going to that house.

When I began to open up and share this incident, I was surprised to find I was not the only one who had been molested. Knowing that others had been through what I been through allowed me the freedom to open up more about it. Still, it was not until I was thirty-nine years old when the Lord told me to tell my mother. I didn't understand why God was now challenging me to share this with my mother, but I believe it was because He was ready to heal this part of my life. At thirty-nine, I was challenged to move past the fear that had developed all those years earlier and speak my truth. I remember saying, "Lord, if this is what You want me to do, You are going to have to help me. You not only have to help me to do this, but You even have to tell me *when* I'm supposed to do this."

I believe secrets keep us in hiding, and we lose a part of our identity when we hide—just like Adam and Eve did in the garden all those millennia ago. The secret they'd attempted to keep was that they had disobeyed God, and it caused them to go into hiding from Him. Withholding secrets from our parents can keep us at a distance from them as well. If we remember that they have been positioned to help keep us safe, we can open up to them about our fears, however big or small they may be.

It took me thirty-one years to realize that I could trust my mother to protect me from my fears. One day, when I was at her house, I felt the little nudging in my spirit that it was time to talk with her. The Lord reminded me of 2 Timothy 1:7, which reads, "For God has not given us a spirit of fear, but of power and of love and of a sound mind." By thirty-nine years old, I decided it was time for me to kick fear out of my life. I prepped my mother by saying, "I have something to tell you, but I need you to know that I am okay. I don't want you to worry or be upset, but I need you to be okay as well."

I began to share with her what had happened to me at eight years old. She was very loving and supportive, and shared with me her own story of trauma. You will never believe it, but as I write this today, on June 29, 2020, I have also told my father that I was sexually abused. I never thought I would tell him.

I share this story with you because, like me, my friends, and even my mother, I know there are many other girls out there who have this same story they have kept secret. My hope is that you will also share your story instead of allowing fear to control you any longer. Come out of hiding and walk in your victory by faith!

2 TIMOTHY 1:7 NKJV

For God has not given us a spirit of fear, but of power and of love and of a sound mind.

THOUGHTS TO CONSIDER

1. Have you ever experienced sexual abuse, and if so, have you told anyone about the incident?
2. If you have not experienced sexual abuse, what are some emotions that came up for you as you read through my story? Empathy? Surprise? Fear? Horror?
3. Do you know anyone personally who may have experienced sexual abuse? How did you feel when they shared their story with you?
4. If you have experienced sexual abuse, did you tell an authority figure who could help you? Why or why not?
5. What is holding you back from getting help or helping a friend find support and therapy?

A PRAYER FOR YOU

Dear God,

Thank You, Lord, for this moment right now, and for every person reading my story. I thank You for Your healing power and Your power of restoration! I thank You for how You see us through some of the most traumatic experiences we may go through. I thank You for being a God that keeps Your Word, for never leaving or forsaking us. I pray for anyone reading this who has experienced any form of sexual abuse. I pray even now, Lord, that You will bring healing to their heart and healing to their mind. Lord, I pray against every spirit of fear, anxiety, shame, and guilt that may have been caused by their abuse.

I pray, even now, that You would encourage each one. Let them know that they are never alone and that You are truly with them through it all. I pray, Lord, that they will release all their hurt and pain to You and that You will wipe away every one of their tears. I pray, Lord, that You will strengthen them, and that they will know their identity and purpose is found in You. I pray even now, oh Lord, that they, too, may have the strength to share their truth, and they will know the Victory that they have in You!

In Jesus' name, amen!

ADDITIONAL SCRIPTURES ON HEALING

Psalm 30:2, Isaiah 53:5, 2 Corinthians 4:8-9, Jeremiah 33:6, 3 John 1:2, Revelation 21:4

THOUGHTS, PRAYERS, & CONVERSATIONS I NEED TO HAVE

_____

_____

A POEM...

the conviction within

BY GINAES' FLOETRY

I could never be forgiven
For this sin
I've trapped myself in.

I'm all tangled up,
Busted and disgusted,
And I don't know what life has for me.
I can't talk to my mama because she would be highly upset with
me.

But, I need to open my mouth because this secret will probably
soon escape,
Because what's done in the dark,
God will surface to light.

And when that happens,
The light will shine and the consequences will be too late.

I'm just so ashamed.
My head is pounding.
My heart is beating like a drum outside my chest.

And my eyes are filled to the overflow with tears.
I'm shaken with fear.
I'm a trembling mess.

I don't even,
I mean,
I can't even,
 trust myself as far as you can throw me.
But even in my bad decision,
Father God,
You are always there to hold me,
To unfold me.

Iron out my wrinkles of imperfection as I try to maintain in my
right mind.
You calm me and still love me even in the worst of times.

I know I've done wrong and I'm so sorry for what I did.
I can't master this alone.
Lord, I need to be freed.
Loose my tongue.

Give me the confidence to have a conversation and, Lord, let my
mother be there for me.
Let her be willing and able.
To sit with me, comfort me, and hold me for awhile,
Because at the end of the day, I'm still her child!

I can do all things through Christ who strengthens me.
I trust you to perform Your Word.
I need my mama during this time of my life.
Please give me the strength, because I need to be heard.

THOUGHTS TO CONSIDER

1. Have you ever had a deep situation, big or small, and needed
   to tell your mama, but felt too ashamed, embarrassed, or
   scared to tell her?
2. What were you afraid of? Her reaction? Disappointing her?
   Losing out on opportunities?
3. What stopped you from telling her?

A POEM...

mother knows

BY GINAES' FLOETRY

I feel a feeling I've never felt before.
Why am I so emotional?
Why are my tears pounding the floor?

It's like something has taken over me.
I'm crying massively for my seed.
The beauty of a mother's connection,
Is that she knows when her child is in need.

What is this Lord?
What am I feeling inside?
It's a strong wave that I can no longer hide.
I can't dodge this if I wanted to, because it's so real.

I can't dismiss this pain in my heart that I really don't want to feel.

But here it is, something You are prepping me for,
So I take this time as You show me what I dread to see.
God it is You who will get me through this indeed.

In Your presence I desire to be.
It's going to take Your strength as You reveal to me,
What's next and the necessary move I have to make?
What help do I offer my child?
What steps do I need to take?

God grant me soft answers and please help me in my response.
Let me be slow to anger, even if my tone may rise.
Let me place myself in her shoes and remember once I was a kid
Who did those things that I can't explain why I did.
Lord, help me to not make my baby feel worse off than she already is.

As I end this prayer with Yes and Amen,
My child comes in with outstretched hands.
Tears are rolling quickly down those puffy cheeks,
As I embrace the face, of stained streaks.

The release, the secret is finally is revealed,
Now we both can work toward being whole and healed.

Lord, I lift the matter of our hearts up to You.
We need You to see us and guide us through.
Thank You that You give just what we need
Small or big on a scale of anything!

THOUGHTS TO CONSIDER

1. Have you ever felt something was off with your child but couldn't put your finger on it?
2. Has God ever shown you signs that you dismissed concerning your child?
3. What steps did you take to uncover the issue?
4. Who do you feel you can confide in and pray with to help you navigate those moments of uncertainty?
5. What kinds of activities can you incorporate into your relationship with your daughter to encourage her to open up more often about hard topics?

PART TWO

conversations from a mama & a mentor

doubt

BY LIV DOOLEY

What is your favorite song? It may share a lot about your heart and your innermost desires. There's a song that came out in 2003 with a few lyrics that say, "I ain't never scared!" Ever heard it? Yea, me neither. Haha! In all seriousness though, this song was one of my favorites when I was a teenager. I shouted, "I ain't never scared," at the top of my lungs with my bass turned all the way up in the Mercedes my Dad let me drive every time I got out of our neighborhood. I danced in the driver seat, nodded my head, and sang at the top of my lungs because I wanted that to be my reality—with everything in me. But the truth is: I was scared.

I was scared of so many different things. There were days during my junior year in high school that I was scared of going to school. I didn't let it show, though. I had a big mouth and I didn't mind demanding that somebody put some respect on my name. Make sense? Not really.

I was scared my parents would find out how hard my year was and pull me out of the school because I didn't want to be *that* girl—the one whose parents had to rescue her again. Make sense? Not really. I was scared that my mentors and youth leaders would find out how depressed or how disrespectful I really was with my mom and how I used alcohol to drown it out. Make sense? Not really.

I was scared my GPA would slip if I let anything get out of hand, so I bottled it in, deflected attention from the real issue, and pushed myself harder. Make sense? Not really. I was scared of not being cute enough, so I binged on Oreo cookies and then starved myself for the rest of the day. I started adding weave to my hair, wearing makeup when my parents let me, and decided to only eat the foods I knew would give me the features the boys liked when I did eat. Make sense? Not really.

I was scared of living. I didn't know what would happen if I kept on. I didn't know if it would get worse. I didn't know if the stress would continue. I didn't know if there was a way out. Make sense?

I was a depressed, yet driven, insecure, yet prideful, fearful, yet bold, little girl who God still called His child, His minister, His teacher. Make sense? Not really. I thank God that the wisdom of the world is foolishness to Him because there is no way in *my* wisdom that *I* would ever have called *me* to the work of the Kingdom of God, and I know I'm not alone. Whether we're thinking of ourselves or the young ladies in our lives, some of us wonder why God would ever choose us because some things just don't make sense.

Does our depression disqualify or discredit us? Nope. Does your daughter's anger alienate her from her calling? Absolutely not. Growing up, I was incredibly protective of my reputation because I refused to let anyone else see the contradictions that I felt deep within me. However, I thank God that He saw everything and still chose to call me. The Word tells us, "Perfect love drives out fear," in 1 John 4:18, and I'm so grateful that His love did just that.

I know you may have a moody teenager on your hands. I know you may have questions about your ability to be used by God when you get tired of your inconsistencies. I know you may want to roll your eyes and walk away when that teenager you've been mentoring ignores all of your advice, but when we feel like we are walking contradictions, we have an opportunity to love. Love who? Love God with all of our hearts, our souls, and our minds. We can love Him enough to ask Him to clear up our inconsistencies. We can love His Word enough to read it over our lives as we remember that there is no fear in love. God says that His strength is perfected in our weaknesses, so He often chooses those of us who are the least likely to serve in His kingdom. That's a reason for a praise break all by itself.

Joshua 3:5 reads, "Joshua told the people, "Consecrate yourselves, for tomorrow the LORD will do amazing things among you." I know there's not much talk about consecration these days, but it is so important to commit every part of ourselves to God. The truth is that this journey we've embraced as

Christians is not about what we *can't* do, but about what we *can* do! We can love the Lord our God with all of our hearts, souls, and minds as we allow the love He has for us and the love we are developing for Him to change our lives. It's God alone who can clear up the inconsistencies and contradictions we feel, so don't let insecurity or the lies of the enemy cause you to hide from His presence and the people He's blessed you to confide in. Consecration will lead you to your best life if you embrace God's Word in the way that you think and the things that you read or watch. Let His Word encourage and transform your friendships. Ask Him to help you expose your fears to those who have the ability to help you.

Pride is your enemy and it is a product of fear—fear of not being enough, fear of not being respected, fear of not being valued. I know you think it's protecting you, but that is a lie. Stop worrying about what others think because it's killing you. It's stealing your joy, it's tormenting your future, and you have to talk to somebody, sis. You have to encourage your daughter to open up. You have to remember that the Bible tells us two are better than one. You have to be the bigger person and get help for yourself, your family, or all of you.

It's easy to run and hide. It's easy to cut people off and push people out. It's easy to give in when your daughter resists going to church or therapy. It's easy to pull the covers up instead of choosing to confront the issue, but you have to. Your choice to consecrate yourself before Jesus will remind you that you have been set apart for a reason, and God will move in even greater ways when you do.

Whether I chose to show up as angry, gifted, intelligent, or temperamental, I had one goal: to maintain my image at all costs... and it almost killed me. You are still called, your daughter is still gifted, and your niece is still blessed. Consecrate yourself and choose to commit to God's will for your life. You'll be surprised by how much freedom you feel in the joy, acceptance, and genuine confidence offered in His presence.

Jeremiah 1:5 tells us that God knew us before we were formed in our mother's bellies. That's true for you, your daughter, and your little sister, but it's time to put in the work to realize the plans God has for us. The work is going to require you to invite God into the messy stuff. The work will lead you to look for wise counsel—people who will not just tell you what you want to hear, but what you *need* to hear. The work is going to make you uncomfortable. The work will remind you to remain humble, but the work is going to bless your whole life! I pray that we let the contradictions in our lives present opportunities to consecrate ourselves to our great Savior, Jesus Christ.

1 JOHN 4:18 NIV

There is no fear in love. But perfect love drives out fear, because fear has to do with punishment. The one who fears is not made perfect in love.

THOUGHTS TO CONSIDER

1. What is one thing you're afraid of right now?
2. How do you downplay your fear or cover it up?
3. What do you think God's Word says about that issue?
4. Find a scripture that will ease that fear in your life and talk about it. Write it on a sticky note, a notebook, or save it as your screensaver.

A PRAYER FOR YOU

Dear God,

In the name of Jesus, I thank You for Your Word! It's Your Word that reminds me You created me in Your image. It's Your Word that reminds me You knew me before I was conceived in my mother's womb. It's Your Word that tells me You have plans for me: plans of peace and not of disaster, to give me a future and a hope. Today, I embrace Your Word for my life. Today, I embrace Your love because I know that it's Your love alone that has the power to drive out the fear that I am not good enough, that my future has been compromised, and that I can't get it together. Your love has the power to change the way I think, the emotions I feel, and the things I believe. I make the decision to humble myself before You so that You can take the reigns. I trust You with my life, my desires, my family, and my future, for You are worthy to be praised.

In Jesus' powerful name I pray, amen.

ADDITIONAL SCRIPTURES ON ASSURANCE

Isaiah 55:11, Psalm 139:16, Jeremiah 1:5, Psalm 51:6,
James 4:8-10, Colossians 1:22, Philippians 3:13-14

THOUGHTS, PRAYERS, & CONVERSATIONS I NEED TO HAVE

_____

_____

_____

_____

_____

_____

_____

_____

insecurity

BY ELIZABETH SANFORD

Is there a lie that the enemy is trying to make you believe about yourself? What self-sabotaging words or mindsets have you spoken over yourself? What can you do to change your psyche about those lies? As I declare that I am fearfully and wonderfully made over and over again, I can remember when I thought it was impossible to believe this about myself. Growing up, I never heard that I was attractive or even lovable. I was not told this.

I do not fault my upbringing. Pouring self-confidence into their eldest child must not have been something my parents felt held high on their priority list. I learned that Biblical principles and the relentless pursuit of educational aspirations were the most important tools for a good life. Today, I still believe this. Learning your place as a Preacher's Kid (PK) was important too. However, building self-esteem was not on the list. They may have assumed it was embedded in the training, but it was not. I grew up as an intelligent little black girl who felt smart, but not beautiful.

I wanted to be beautiful. I wanted to feel beautiful. I wanted to look like the girls I so admired—the ones the boys drooled over. I wanted long, wavy hair with flawless skin, but my hair was short and kinky. Black marks and darkened patches graced my cheeks and chin. Pressing combs and perms were used to straighten my hair. I had acne, blackheads, and scars where the pimples had been. I felt ugly and I believed I was. People used to snicker behind my back or turn their nose up in my face and say how ugly I was, and I agreed. I inhaled every aspect of ugliness.

What did I do? I attempted to find my worth in pleasing people. I became the ultimate people pleaser. In my mind, if people liked me, I was worthy. I complied with just about everything asked of me. I did not think I was worthy of having an opinion. I believed ugly people took whatever they could get. I thought that if I could make them happy, they would see how beautiful I was. I just wanted to hear someone say I was pretty, I was beautiful. I thought hearing this would mean that I could be loved, because no one loves an ugly person.

The rejection in my relationships felt like it was directly connected to my appearance. I never let people see how hurt or lonely I really felt, but many nights, I cried myself to sleep.

One day, God spoke with me. His gentle words rang out so sweetly in my ears, "You are beautiful. Very beautiful."

Me? Beautiful? Yeah, right! What? Nope!

I refused to receive it at first, but His words kept repeating like the steady beat of a drum, "You are beautiful. Very Beautiful." Tears began to flow like a cleansing, gentle rain. As I internalized this idea, the words began to wash away the pain, the agony, the sadness, the melancholy, the disapproving murmurings, and the hurtful words that were spoken aloud in my mind and in public concerning me.

God continued to remind me of these words. One day, I heard Joel Osteen declare, "You are fearfully and wonderfully made." Peace settled in my gut. It stopped me in my tracks! I couldn't believe it was scripture, so I searched for it, and I found it in Psalm 139:14. It reads: "I praise you because I am fearfully and wonderfully made. Your works are wonderful, I know that full well." Immediately, I became determined to make this my new battle cry!

Those healing words gave me the strength to stand against the broken record of low self-esteem, negativity, and self-hatred that played over and over, well into my adult years (until my mid-forties, to be exact). After decades of holding my head down, I began to walk with my head held high. Those healing words allowed me to begin to avert the ever-rising tide of negativity and self-hatred. I found rest in, "You are beautiful. Very beautiful. You are fearfully and wonderfully made." Those affirming words gave me life.

I stood in the mirror daily, repeating, "I am beautiful, very beautiful. I am fearfully and wonderfully made. God said it. I rest in this." It was a serious struggle at first. An affirmation and declaration will not erase the decades of negativity in one day. I kept pushing, believing, and seeking the beauty in the mirror that God said was there. The struggle was real. There were times I could not bear to see myself. I didn't feel it, I didn't see it, so how could I possibly believe it? Jesus told us that, "The spirit is willing, but the flesh is weak." There were times when I would break down crying in the mirror as my mind attempted to convince me of the words I spoke. However, I was determined to change my mindset about myself. I could not take the negativity I held like a cozy, comfortable blanket any longer. I had to let it go. The mirror affirmations became my daily ritual, and I kept fighting until I believed it with every beat of my heart. "I am beautiful. I am very beautiful. I am fearfully and wonderfully made."

I am here to decree, affirm, and declare that every woman, regardless of age, race, creed, color, religious or spiritual beliefs, is beautiful. If you don't believe you're beautiful, you never feel beautiful when you look in the mirror, you have never thought of yourself as desirable, or you have suffered from low self-esteem and self-hatred, I want to repeat that **you are beautiful**! Everything about you is beautiful! Your eyes, your lips, the shape of your nose, your gorgeous skin tone, your perfectly chiseled face, your hair, your physique, and your absolutely gorgeous smile that brings pure joy to all you meet. Your body shape and type are beautiful! Your personality is beautiful! Everything about you is beautiful! The Lord, your God, says, "You are altogether beautiful, my darling: there is no flaw in you. Yes, you are beautiful, very beautiful! You are fearfully and wonderfully made."

Am I concerned about my appearance? Yes, of course. Who isn't? Am I concerned with adult acne? Yes. It is an indication that my diet needs an adjustment. Do I fuss over my hair? Yes. I still can't make up my mind to keep or cut my locs. Am I dogging myself with thoughts and words of negativity? I can honestly say "Nope!" Though my past makes its attempts to haunt me with its untruth, I know that is just what it is. It is an *untruth* engineered by the enemy to stop the awesome things God has for me. This is my real truth: I am beautiful, inside and out—perceived flaws and all. I am fearfully and wonderfully made. I am at peace with God's creation. Thank God for the person who said, "God never made junk," because it's true for both of us!

PSALM 139:14 NIV

I praise you because I am fearfully and wonderfully made; your works are wonderful, I know that full well.

THOUGHTS TO CONSIDER

1. What self-sabotaging words or mindsets have you spoken over yourself. What have you had to overcome?

2. What is the hardest thing to accept about yourself, be it your appearance or your personality?

3. What affirmations of self-worth have you stood in the mirror and poured into yourself lately?

A PRAYER FOR YOU

Dear Heavenly Father,

I thank You for Your loving kindness and tender faithfulness towards me. I thank You, Father God, for Your outstretched hand of deliverance from the negative thoughts that once gripped me with turmoil, anxiety, and torment. Thank You for breaking the chains of low self-esteem, low self-worth, and repeated self-hatred that once plagued me. Thank You, Father God, for destroying the blanket of negativity that previously wrapped me in its grip. You broke the yoke of thinking I must live up to the standards of someone else's beauty and of people's approval. You saved me from people. You saved me from myself.

I thank You for calling me beautiful, for making me see my worth. You declared I was fearfully and wonderfully made. You affirmed I am altogether beautiful; I have no flaws. I believe the report of The Lord. I now have beauty for ashes and joy for mourning. I thank You, Dear Father, for being the lifter of my head, my mind, my heart, and my spirit through Jesus Christ. I thank You, Father God, for loving me to see my beautiful self. You loved me back to life. I give You the glory, the honor, and the praise.

In Jesus' name, amen.

ADDITIONAL SCRIPTURES ON BEAUTY

Genesis 1:27, Ephesians 2:10, Song of Songs 4:1, Isaiah 62:3
Proverbs 31:30, Psalm 27:4

THOUGHTS, PRAYERS, & CONVERSATIONS
I NEED TO HAVE

_____

_____

_____

_____

_____

_____

_____

_____

perfectionism

BY KELLY FOSTER

When you were a little girl, did you ever dream your life would end up like this? Did your dreams of the future ever whisk you away to a faraway place where there were no money problems, fights between parents, or rowdy kids? As a child, did you envision your life as a place of peace and perfection? I did. I was that dreamer, that little girl who hoped that every dream she dreamt as a child would manifest itself in the future, creating a picture-perfect image of true love. True love, as I thought, was ultimately personified when a man chose a woman as his wife, and they bore the fruit of that love through the birth of their children. Yep, that was true love. And then they lived happily ever after...

You can imagine my delight when I was "chosen" by a charming man, and he took my hand in marriage. Our love overflowed as our home grew with not one, but three, beautiful little girls—little mini me's in the making. The newness of my responsibilities was exciting, and the challenges were well worth it. It was my badge of honor. I was who I had always wanted to be: a wife and mother loved by her family and doted over publicly. The only problem was that the beautiful dream I had of motherhood was quickly overshadowed by sleepless nights, fatigue, and what felt like endless standards to keep up with.

Trouble in my marriage was followed by financial struggles, bankruptcy, and unemployment. Women are challenged with working, bearing children, raising them with love and respect, and staying fit (which always includes back" to your pre-pregnancy size—quickly, of course). Women are pressured to stay educated—financially, politically, and socially —and, somehow, find time to take care of themselves. It's a lot.

When my dream began to crumble, I found myself drowning in a sea of shame, caused by a childhood full of unrealistic dreams, issues with perfectionism, and lies from the enemy. I finally recognized it while sitting on a mountain of laundry in my living room. I remember crying out to the Lord with tears streaming down my face, "This is not the way it's supposed to be. This is not the life of my dreams." God spoke to me through His Word, "Fear not, for I have redeemed you. I have called you by name. You are mine. When you pass through the waters, I will be with you, and through the rivers, they shall not overwhelm you; when you walk through the fire, you shall not be burned, and the flame shall not consume you" (Isaiah 43:1b-2).

God often speaks to us through the Bible, and when I read it, God placed the impression of His Word on my heart. When I listened to God and allowed Him to open my eyes and remove the veil of fantasy that clouded my vision, I realized my problems were not the issues in my marriage or my picky-eating, bickering children. My problems were not my lack of energy or money. My problem—and, I suspect, your problem, too—began a long time ago, before motherhood. Before the titles mother, wife, employee, student, or friend labeled us, we had a problem. Our problem arose when someone tried to convince us that life is a dream, bad things never happen to good people, and all we need is the validation of a man, a job, a family, a career, or a label to make us who we want to be. They promised that, with these things, we would be happy.

Ladies, this is the biggest lie our adversary tries to taunt us with. Let's start combatting this lie with the declaration: I am not perfect, but I am His. Although my perfectly curated Instagram didn't show it, my insecurity, lack of self-worth, pride, envy, and discontentment was very present amid the pretty pink and green branded photos. But God. Just when we get to the point where we feel like we can't take it anymore, God steps in to crush the lies and restore balance. Despite all the lies, I believed God was ever-present. The Creator of the universe corrected my misguided and jaded heart.

Today, God wants to rid you and me of every shame, fear of failure, and guilt we may have and replace it with His freely-given, immeasurable love. He loves us, and we are His. This truth is unshaken by any circumstance life throws our way. The love of Christ has carried me through the fire of mom shame, the gut-wrenching pain of betrayal in my marriage, and the brokenness of unfulfilled dreams. God's love has comforted me, encouraged me, and has been faithful to remove my faulty thinking about life. He's replaced those naive, worldly, self-centered, and ungodly lies with the limitless truth of His love for me, and He will do the same for you.

Jesus wants to offer you the same love, compassion, forgiveness, and gift of rest that He gave to me. No matter what waters you go through or what lies you believe, God is eagerly waiting to be your redeemer. He has chosen you, and that fact will never change. Life is not about being perfect, having a beautiful family, a great job, or a small waistline. God actually wants to use your imperfections to shine a light on His perfect glory.

If you are struggling with the constant demands of all the hats and labels you wear, remember God's words, "My grace is all you need. My power works best in weakness. So now I am glad to boast about my weaknesses so that the power of Christ can work through me" (2 Corinthians 12:9). God promises to take care of us, be with us, and sustain us despite our broken dreams. Our identities are found in Christ alone, and in His presence, we can lay every burden of this world down and embrace the freedom of His unfailing love.

2 CORINTHIANS 12:9 NIV

But he said to me, "My grace is sufficient for you, for my power is made perfect in weakness." Therefore I will boast all the more gladly about my weaknesses, so that Christ's power may rest on me.

THOUGHTS TO CONSIDER

1. How have your dreams of the life you wanted kept you from embracing the life that you have?
2. What people, ideas, or concepts do you seek validation from instead of trusting God's words?
3. What burdens of your life can you lay at the feet of Jesus right now, and in exchange, pick up God's freely given love?

A PRAYER FOR YOU

Dear Jesus,

Thank You, God, for calling me Your beloved, Your most precious and cherished one. Help me to see myself as You see me. Help me to embrace the identity I have in You and to abandon anything that speaks against that. Guide me by the power of Your Holy Spirit to live the life that You have set before me; embracing the good with the bad, the ups and the downs, and the seasons of sowing and reaping, knowing that You work all things together for my good. Lord, help me to no longer be a slave to perfectionism, cynicism, and people-pleasing, but rather that I find rest in You and Your perfect peace daily. As I see myself how You see me, God, may it spill over into every area of my life, impacting my family, children, spouse, and friends.

In Jesus' name I pray, amen.

ADDITIONAL SCRIPTURES ON TRUST in god

Hebrews 13:8, Proverbs 16:3, Psalm 32:8, Isaiah 54:10, Psalm 118:8, James 1:2-4

THOUGHTS, PRAYERS, & CONVERSATIONS I NEED TO HAVE

_____

_____

_____

_____

_____

A CONVERSATION ON ...

disobedience

BY ZATOYIA JONES-COLQUITT

Have you ever heard the still, small voice of God telling you to do something that you chose to ignore? What were the consequences?

I missed out on the mental clarity, the direction, and the ability to obey God's still small, still voice. I missed it all due to disobedience.

The first time I heard God speak to my heart and say, "Let it go," I ignored it and got fired! So, I did what I did best at the time: questioned my understanding, ignored His voice, and found a new job. The money was good, and the title felt big, so I thought I deserved it. After all, I was a confident, committed, reliable, and hardworking quality employee with two master's degrees. Everything I put my hands to was successful, so I decided I had misheard God say, "Let it go." Forget that other company. This new position was God's best for me.

But it wasn't. God was telling me to rest, but honestly, I did not know what that meant. I had been working since I was fifteen years old, and now that I was a single parent of two in a brand-new house with the responsibilities to accompany them, I felt accountable to my work. I couldn't let go. What would that mean? You see, work was where I found my meaning. It kept me out of trouble. It motivated me. It allowed me to provide for my family and take care of us with a single mother's paycheck. It provided an escape from the emotional trauma of my past experiences that I'd worked so hard to ignore. You know the trauma—disappointment, heartache, physical abuse, mental abuse, bullying. Work supported me in more ways than one.

As it turned out, the new position I ran to brought along its own set of problems. Anxiety weighed heavily on me because I had not taken the time to rest and heal from my previous experience. In addition to that, I had to deal with other people's emotional issues, and it felt like everyone wanted me to solve their problem. I gave until I had nothing left to give. I gave until my eyelids closed involuntarily. I gave until I felt like I was running on fumes. I gave until the burnout stripped me of confidence in my own abilities. I gave until I could no longer see my worth. I gave until my best was no longer my best. I gave until heaviness crushed me and I had no choice but to cover my ears and cry out, "God, help me!" He did. He forced me to rest.

Disobedience can steal your mind, your thoughts, and your emotions. It can take away your vision. It leaves you feeling devalued and unappreciated. It leaves you burnt out. It erodes your trust. It draws you away from prayer and people, and it isolates you. But God! God gave me another chance to come and rest in Him, to be restored and recharged for the next level.

Being fired inevitably tainted my ego and made me question all of my skills, but all God wanted me to do was trust Him and rest. His Word says, "Come to me, all you who are weary and burdened, and I will give you rest" (Matthew 11:28-30). Trust and rest were a learning experience for me. I was used to being the teacher and the leader. This time, I had to rely on someone else's guidance. I had to rely on Him to teach me how to rest and trust Him with my every move. In Luke 15:3-7, the scripture talks about how He left the ninety-nine to find the lost one. I was that one He found. God loved me so much, He did not want me to be left behind. He knew me before I was formed in my mother's womb (Jeremiah 1:5). Once I rested and put my trust in Him, I was able to draw closer to Him. Rest gave me peace of mind and clarity. The steps on the pages were no longer blank.

God really wants the best for you; He wants His rest for you. To enter into God's rest, you must trust in Him and repent for your disobedience. Don't allow disobedience to isolate you, harden your heart, and pull you away from God. When you trust God and believe what His Word says, you can find the rest and peace of mind you need to walk in the purpose He has for you.

LUKE 15:3-7 NIV

Jesus told this parable: "Suppose one of you has a hundred sheep and loses one of them. Doesn't he leave the ninety-nine in the open country and go after the lost sheep until he finds it? And when he finds it, he joyfully puts it on his shoulders and goes home. Then he calls his friends and neighbors together and says, 'Rejoice with me; I have found my lost sheep.' I tell you that in the same way there will be more rejoicing in heaven over one sinner who repents than over ninety-nine righteous persons who do not need to repent."

THOUGHTS TO CONSIDER

1. Are you burnt out emotionally?
2. Are you looking for rest and peace of mind?
3. How have you missed God due to disobedience?

A PRAYER FOR YOU

Father God,

Because of Your grace, I can bring all my burdens of disappointment, heartache, anxiety, hurt, pain, and emotional burnout to You. Forgive me for my disobedience and not following Your lead. Forgive me for thinking I knew what was best for me and straying away from You trying to fix and rely on my own understanding. Thank You for coming back for me.

Thank You for healing me. Thank You for restoring me. Thank You that I can lean on and trust in You knowing that You will guide me to fulfill the purpose You destined for me before I was born. I believe what Your Word says about me. I am healed and will walk in purpose!

In Jesus' name I pray, amen.

ADDITIONAL SCRIPTURES ON OBEDIENCE

Ephesians 2:8-9, 1 Samuel 15:22, Philippians 2:8, Luke 11:28, Hebrews 3:15, John 10:27, 1 John 3:24

THOUGHTS, PRAYERS, & CONVERSATIONS I NEED TO HAVE

_____

_____

_____

_____

_____

_____

_____

distraction

BY BEVERLY YOUNG

Can you recall the most cherished moment of your life? The time, the place, the people? How would you feel if you had missed it and you couldn't get it back? How can you replace, recapture, or relive that moment?

I'm ashamed to admit it, but there was a time when I didn't value my mother for who she was. I was a teenager and I didn't want to be anything like her. She was the cook. She always cooked a full dinner with sides. I didn't want fried chicken and greens, mashed potatoes and gravy, or those yeast rolls, bread pudding, or sweet potato pies. She was the hairdresser who combed my hair every day before I went to elementary school and who pressed and curled my hair for picture day. She was the housekeeper and the landlord. Oh, how I hated those hardwood floors. All of my friends had new carpet on their living room floors. I didn't want to learn to cook, wash the dishes, or keep the house clean. I just wanted to work and earn money to buy what *I* wanted to buy. I couldn't wait until my sixteenth birthday so I could get a job. I wanted a professional life. I was selfish and condescending to my mother and I didn't think very much of her life. I didn't see what God had blessed me with. It wasn't until I was older that I realized her life was all about her family. I didn't take time to become the daughter that God had created me to be.

I became the adult, got married, and had you five years later. Unfortunately, my mind was still in my career. Again, I didn't see what God had blessed me with. I did not value the sacred time I had with you. I spent my young adulthood rushing through your adolescent, tween, and teenage years with busyness, always striving for more. An associate's degree, a bachelor's degree, and a master's degree were not enough. I had to enroll in a Ph.D. program. I became a teacher and a coordinator for a nationally accredited after-school program. I was promoted to principal, and, of course, before I completed the Ph.D., I became superintendent.

All of those classes and meetings I attended made me feel like I was "somebody", but that was a trick of the evil one; I already was "somebody". I am YOUR mother, a wife, a daughter, a sister, and above all, a child of The Most High God. I was totally confused, and my priorities were mixed up! Chasing education and a career just added stress and further drained my energy, which took away from the time I should have devoted to you. Yes, we had some fun times—the weekend movies with popcorn and bike riding were our favorites—but the amount of quality family time was out of balance with the time I devoted to work and education. I didn't give our family or you what you deserved.

Then the cycle repeated itself. You started counting the days until you would be leaving to go to college. You couldn't wait to get out of the house. You got your bachelor's degree, a master's degree, became a teacher, began volunteering, started an organization for girls, and became an author. Don't get me wrong—I am proud of you. Education and career are important, but ministry begins at home. God gives us choices and He also gives us the desires of our hearts, but it's up to us to place priorities on the most important things. I learned this lesson later in life, but I believe you will discover it faster than I did. Trust God! Jeremiah 29:11 reads, "For I know the plans I have for you," says the Lord. "They are plans for good and not for disaster, to give you a future and a hope."

COVID-19 has given us a reset button. It has allowed us to bring family to the forefront and put jobs, education, and organizations in second place. This is a different way of life for us. I noticed that you choose busyness too. I know that you love the Lord and that He loves you. He has begun a great work in you, and He will complete it. Give God your schedule and your calendar. One completed item from God's list is greater than ten completed things from your list. Psalms 139:23-24 says, "Search me, O God, and know my heart; test me and know my anxious thoughts. Point out anything in me that offends you, and lead me along the path of everlasting life."

The time is now for you to live those cherished moments in real-time. Prioritize them, rather than trying to replace or relive them later. Oh, how I wish that I had worked alongside mom in the kitchen, learning to bake that bread whose aroma filled the house. If only I had those beautifully varnished and dusted hardwood floors. I am grateful that God allowed me to appreciate and value my mother and tell her how much I loved her before she passed away. I told mom, "God could have birthed me in another country or continent to a different mother, but I am so happy that He chose you to be my mother." I take comfort in knowing I had the opportunity to tell her how I felt. I'm glad I had the chance to replace those actions and attitudes I exhibited when I lived at home with loving and caring words of affection.

Thirty-three years have passed in a blink since you were born! So I say to you, "I am so blessed that God gave me you as a daughter, and He has allowed me to see you grow into a beautiful, caring young woman. I am so proud of who you are. I love the way our relationship has blossomed and I am grateful for this opportunity to tell you I love you!" Enjoy every season, accept each day as a gift from God. Don't question God's plan, just ask Him to give you the faith and strength to stay in it.

PSALM 139: 1,24 NIV

You have searched me, Lord, and you know me.
See if there is any offensive way in me, and lead me in the way everlasting.

THOUGHTS TO CONSIDER

1. Do I pray first, asking God His plan for my life, and do I wait for His answer?
2. How can I include and consider my immediate family's feelings about my goals?
3. Do I take time daily for prayer, my family, and health (eating and exercise)?
4. Do I leave natural breaks within my daily schedule (morning, lunch, and afternoon) and time to gather my thoughts, rather than schedule back to back meetings and appointments?
5. Do I schedule an eight-hour day or do I make appointments from morning until late into the evening?
6. Did I take a break after achieving a goal before starting another major goal (like another degree)?

A PRAYER FOR YOU

Dear God,

Please forgive me for being selfish with my time. Please help me to live in the moment and to enjoy the dreams of my family. Please help me to pray with my family and enjoy fun activities together. Please help me to value each day and plan each day together. Please show me how to press into You. Please help me to remember that You have plans for me. Thank You for the thoughts You have for me. Please help me to walk in the blessings You bestow on me. Please speak Your words into my life. Please give me Your words to speak. Thank You for being with me always, no matter what. Please help me to be a blessing to others!

In Jesus' name, amen!

ADDITIONAL SCRIPTURES ON INTENTIONALITY

Luke 10:40-42, 1 Corinthians 13:2, Galatians 5:22-23,
1 Thessalonians 5:16-18, Psalm 32:8, 1 John 4:12,
Hebrews 13:1-2

THOUGHTS, PRAYERS, & CONVERSATIONS I NEED TO HAVE

_____

_____

_____

_____

_____

_____

_____

regret

BY DECEMBER JAMES

Do you know the difference between a superhero and a human mother? The expectations are about the same, except moms don't have extraordinary powers. Think about it—we expect moms to save the world, capture villains, and morph into superheroes, all while cooking dinner. The reality is we will never meet those demands because being human parents means we are going to make human mistakes.

At twenty-five, I was a recent grad from Idaho State University and a new resident of Las Vegas, Nevada. I got my first salaried job and began dating a man who was charming and very handsome. The fact that he was forty was not important to me at the time. He would leave town for weeks and then show up to spend the night with me for two or three days. During that time, he would often pay my bills and take me out to eat. I thought nothing of it. Honestly, just believing this older man liked me was thrilling. One weekend, my mom came to visit my sister and me. I was eager for my boyfriend and mother to meet, but when my mom asked him, "What does a forty-year-old want with a twenty-five-year-old?" I began to spiral back into the dance my mother and I had engaged in since my birth.

I am the eldest of three daughters. My mother got pregnant with me at sixteen. She was in high school living with my grandparents—who were considered pastors—so you can imagine that my introduction into this world and our relational journey was a strange one. In my earliest memories, I can recount moments that she would try to engage with me and I would reject her, or times I tried to connect with her, and she would dismiss) me. By the time I was a senior in high school, I despised my mom and I began counting the days until I could move out. When she suddenly showed interest and care in the man I was dating at twenty-five, I was surprised, confused, embarrassed, and, yes, angry! Always angry.

One day, Mom did something so powerful. She sent her twenty-five-year-old daughter a letter—a letter that I still have today. This letter was filled with hurtful truths and healing revelations. Mom began the letter by listing my accomplishments and proud moments, indicating how present she was during peak moments in my life. Then, she shared the hard truth—the truth I had felt my entire life—that no one else had been able to see but me. I was her shame, and she had raised me as her shame.

The reason for her letter was to apologize for those feelings, but, more importantly, to display a hope that I would not ruin my life with this forty-year-old drug dealer and pimp. My mom wanted me to know I was worth so much more than what he was offering. I cried in silence. Sitting there, feeling everything that letter was meant to bring: correction, healing, concern, and, most of all, love.

A month later, I dumped that guy after discovering his week-long absences were (in fact) due to him smuggling drugs across the border and taking women with him to serve as accomplices, should he ever be caught. I realized he was grooming me to be one of these women. To this day, I've never spoken a word about the letter to my mother or told her about that guy's intentions for me, either.

Now that I am a mother, I have thought several times about how hard it must have been for my mother to write that letter to her very defensive, overly sensitive, misunderstood, hurting daughter. I've often thought about how my mom had everything to lose in sending me that letter. She laid her ego and her pride down, and she risked the little relationship we did have left to ensure that I would not suffer the cost of this mistake. See, in that moment, my mom did not wear a cape or a mask, nor did she have extraordinary powers. She was simply being the mother I needed at that time—open, honest, sacrificial, and vulnerable.

Like mothers everywhere, I understand how our children are our hearts and how they tug at our souls. We are busy balancing our careers, cloaking our shame, and hiding our mistakes while caring for their physical needs. We often neglect and forget that children have emotional developmental needs, because we're trying so hard to hold it all together ourselves— like superheroes.

The Gospel of Mark says, "For whosoever will save his life shall lose it, but whosoever shall lose his life for my sake and the Gospel's shall save it. For what shall it profit a man, if he shall gain the whole world, and lose his own soul?" And so I ask, what profits a mother to save face, ascend the corporate ladder with increased salaries and storied accomplishments, only to lose her daughters? God gave us our daughters. As we raise them, tough things will happen., some of which will be too shameful to revisit or even mention because... that's life.

Remembering traumatic events from your childhood or your formative stages through your adult lens can allow you to rationalize and navigate your way through them emotionally. Can our daughters do the same? Some of the hurts they will experience will be caused by you, even though pain and suffering were not your intent. Who gives permission to talk about the unspoken? Who offers that safe place to speak? Will it arrive in a letter when she is twenty-five years old, or will it be on the family room couch when she's twelve? Find time to talk about the hard stuff. Lay down your life to save hers.

MARK 8:35 NIV

For whoever wants to save their life will lose it, but whoever loses their life for me and for the gospel will save it.

THOUGHTS TO CONSIDER

1. Do you have "mom" time? Designate a time where your daughter can ask you things, say what's on her mind, or be just herself with your undivided attention. Ask tough questions and listen without judgment.
2. Take an honest assessment of your relationship with your daughter and consider family therapy. Therapy can be a safe place for you and your daughter to reshape and reconcile the bond that God intended when He formed you two together.
3. Buy a journal and write a letter to your daughter. Then, give her the journal and ask her to write a letter to you. Keep this letter-journaling alive as your daughter ages. See if your relationship grows stronger with each passing year.

A PRAYER FOR YOU

God of heaven and earth,

I thank You for this opportunity to build a solid relationship with my daughter starting today. I thank You, Father, for healing our journey and for forgiving me for not always doing things in order. God, You are the superhero, and I put my faith and trust in You that You will give me the strength, wisdom, and creativity to connect with my daughter at all stages of her life. I ask for longevity in my bond with my daughter and that our relationship be an example and ministry to others. I pray for my daughter's heart to be healed from the pain of my mistakes and misunderstandings. I thank You, Father, for giving us a safe place to have the hard, healing, and much needed conversations in order to grow and go forward. Order our steps and guide our words.

In the mighty name of Jesus, amen.

ADDITIONAL SCRIPTURES ON APPRECIATION

Isaiah 43:18-19, Romans 8:28, 1 John 3:20, John 10:10, Romans 5:8, 2 Corinthians 7:10, Philippians 2:4

THOUGHTS, PRAYERS, & CONVERSATIONS I NEED TO HAVE

_____

_____

_____

_____

_____

disappointment

BY JENNIFER SHUMAKER

Have you ever been disappointed in life? Have you hoped or expected for something to happen only to find it didn't? How do you work through disappointment?

Life is full of disappointments, but how we deal with them is what makes all the difference. I have had many disappointments in my life, so I can relate to not knowing how to deal with them. I used to deal with them by putting up walls and separating myself from others, which made me feel like I had no one to turn to. I now realize that what I was really feeling was rejected by the people in my life.

One day, I met a friend named Jesus. As I grew in the Word, I discovered that He accepted me when everyone else rejected me. I could lean on Him. Being in relationship with

Jesus didn't mean I wouldn't experience disappointments, but I now had a friend who would help me through them.

I distinctly recall two disappointments in my life that led me closer to Jesus. The first was in my marriage. I thought I married my best friend, but soon realized that we weren't as close as I'd imagined. I felt betrayed by him. The second biggest disappointment of my life was when my oldest son went back to jail. It pierced me to my soul and left me feeling as if death had come to my home. I couldn't understand how this could happen to me again. The disappointment robbed me of my peace and left me with no appetite. Recovering from these disappointments was difficult, but I had to learn to make my peace with them. Since then, I've learned to take one day at a time and let tomorrow take care of itself.

I'm so grateful I met a friend named Jesus. As I grew in the Word, I found I had Jesus to lean on during my greatest disappointments, and He helped me get through them all. Through Christ, I have been able to live with expectation again. I know disappointment is part of life, but we have to believe God's Word and trust in Him to heal us. 2 Corinthians 4:8-9 lets us know that things do happen in life, but it also reminds us that God will never leave us, and we can make it through as long as we stick with Him. It reads, "We are troubled on every side, yet not distressed; we are perplexed, but not in despair."

When you are facing disappointments, remember my story. I had to grow closer to Jesus to overcome the disappointments I experienced. I knew that satan, the enemy, was trying to destroy my family and steal our souls. If we are not careful, we can become oblivious to satan's attacks. Don't lose your perspective. The Bible tells us, "The thief cometh not, but for to steal, and to kill, and to destroy: I have come that they might have life and that they might have it more abundantly" (John 10:10 KJV).

We have to learn how to pray and seek God for our healing. God truly wants us to have a prosperous life. With His help, we can get through anything, but we have to believe it! We have to work to overcome our disappointments and not allow satan to use them against us or cause us to take our focus off of God's plan for our lives.

But make sure you read the whole scripture. Jesus says, "I am come that they might have life and that they might have it more abundantly." When I look up the word abundantly, it means that God wants us to have plenty of everything we need. He wants us to have plenty of joy, peace, and love. This scripture reveals that no matter how many disappointments may come our way, God wants us to have the best.

Despite all of my disappointments, I still believe that God wants me to have a life of joy and hope. I have learned that without God's Word, I cannot stand. Allow God's Word to hold you up through all of your disappointments.

The scripture tells us that God is always with us. Though we may face a lot of hurt and persecution in life, He will not forsake us. We will not be cast down, we will not be destroyed, and we don't have to give up. To receive my breakthrough, I had to seek God. As I sought the Lord for an answer, I had to take one day at a time. We can't worry about the past. We have to deal with the present and let God take care of the future. I had to learn to put all my trust in God, and so do you. We have to believe just what the Word of God says and always remember, "I can do all things through Christ which strengtheneth me" (Philippians 4:13).

2 CORINTHIANS 4:8-9 NIV

We are hard pressed on every side, but not crushed; perplexed, but not in despair; persecuted, but not abandoned; struck down, but not destroyed.

THOUGHTS TO CONSIDER

1. What are some of your life's disappointments?
2. How do you plan to deal with them?
3. Who are you confiding in for help?
4. What types of things help you remain hopeful in this season?
5. Be mindful about your conversation during this time and pray about everything.

A PRAYER FOR YOU

Lord,

I thank You, Father God, for this day and I thank You, Lord God, for being with me as I go through disappointments in my life. I know, Lord, that You are always and forever present in my life, but Lord, You know sometimes, as we go through disappointments, our thoughts of You can be so far away. Lord, I ask You to help me when I am in a way of unbelief or not understanding. Lord, I know whatever I go through that You have an abundant plan for my life. So I ask You for Your strength, Lord, as I go through this situation, and I ask You for Your help. You say in Your Word that when I am weak, You are strong. Lord, You are my strength and my refuge. My trust is in You, Lord Jesus. So I ask you Lord, once again, to help me through this disappointment and I will be forever grateful to You, Lord.

In Jesus of Nazareth's name I pray, amen.

ADDITIONAL SCRIPTURES ON HOPE

Psalm 13:12, Lamentations 3:21-24, Hebrews 6:19-20, Matthew 6:34, 2 Corinthians 4:8-9, 1 Peter 1:13, Hebrews 10:23, Isaiah 40:31

THOUGHTS, PRAYERS, & CONVERSATIONS I NEED TO HAVE

_____

_____

_____

_____

_____

_____

_____

_____

_____

_____

_____

_____

_____

_____

_____

loss

BY LESLEE ROGERS

Have you experienced a profound loss in your life? To whom or what did you turn for solace and comfort?

I met my Ron early in 1988 at a business luncheon. We met again several months later and had our first date the next evening, which was the beginning of our whirlwind romance. Several weeks later, we were engaged, and four and a half months after that first date, we were married—my first marriage, his second! This may not be the right path for every couple, but at thirty-seven and forty-one, it was the right path for us. We knew we were meant for one another! We planned to be happily married for fifty years and would have been, but God had other plans.

Just before Ron's sixty-seventh birthday, he was diagnosed with stage 4, inoperable cancer. Ron's initial response to that diagnosis was, "Why not me?" As Ron reminded me, Jesus' followers have bad things happen to them too; we are not exempt from them just because He lives in our heart.

He surprised me by adding, "This is a win-win—if I survive, I get to stay with you, and if I don't, I get to be with Jesus!"

I reminded him that it would only be a win-win for him, because I would be left alone. He looked stricken when I said that, but I told him that if the roles were reversed, I would feel exactly the way he did. That made him feel better.

We began the good fight from the onset. Ron had chemotherapy treatments, and people watched how he responded to his circumstances, amazing us all. He continued to teach about Jesus and how He changes the lives of those who surrender to Him. Even after he left his job, he continued to share his take on the Word via Facebook, affecting change in people as the cancer made changes in him.

We had sixteen months from that first diagnosis and we shared twenty-seven years—not the fifty we initially hoped for. I was bereft, lonely, heartbroken. But my husband, the pastor, also taught me well, and so I knew I would never truly be alone despite how I might feel in the moment. *The presence of the Lord isn't a feeling, but it is a fact we can embrace as our truth in every season.*

We all must walk the path of grief that comes with loss in our own way and at our own pace—there is definitely no one-size-fits-all way to experience grief and loss. For me, survival was achieved by noting all the firsts in the year following the loss as they passed. You know the firsts: Christmas and New

Year's (which came right after Ron died), all the ensuing holidays and birthdays, the first time you roll over and put your hand out to an empty side of the bed, and the first dinner out alone. Once all those "firsts" had passed, I felt like it was time to move forward a bit, and for me, that was expressed by moving my wedding ring to my right hand. My way is certainly not everyone's way, but the truth is: grief is a very important process in life. It has to be experienced following a loss. However, it should never take over and control a person's life. We should only relinquish control to the One who knows us best and wants the best for us!

At some time in our lives, we all come face to face with the loss of someone we love dearly—a parent, our spouse and/or life partner, a child, a close friend, or even a dream we planned our life around. Questioning God—even getting angry with God—in these difficult times, is simply a part of our human nature. However, those of us blessed with a relationship with Jesus do not simply abide in our humanness, because we are becoming more like Christ every day. The human part of us that produces anger is best served when we allow the Holy Spirit in us to have control, all the while, dissipating that anger.

We have Jesus to rely on when we can't sleep, think we can't breathe, and can't consider living our lives as if nothing has changed. For us, EVERYTHING has changed! Focusing on the strength Jesus provides takes our eyes off of *what* we have lost and puts it squarely on W*ho* we have to get us from one moment to the next until we emerge from those depths.

As it is written in 2 Corinthians 1:4, "He comes along-side us when we go through hard times, and before you know it, he brings us alongside someone else who is going through hard times so that we can be there for that person just as God was there for us."

When we think we cannot put one foot in front of the other, that is the time to take a look around. We can often find someone who is suffering even more than we are. If you only have the opportunity to offer a hug and a simple, "I can only imagine how you feel," do it! Taking ourselves out of our own misery to be available to someone else can totally change our perspective. Yes, we still hurt and we still cry alone in bed at night, but realizing we are not the only ones living with grief allows the heartache to lessen just enough to help us take a deep breath. Just as God has provided the Comforter for us, we, in turn, must become a comforter to others if we want to get out from under the burden that grief and loss can place on us.

Allow the strength and love that comes from Jesus alone help you be the strength and love for someone else. Only then will you realize that although we may have to suffer as Jesus suffered, we also will be able to rejoice in the good times that still await us!

2 CORINTHIANS 1:3-4 NIV

Praise be to the God and Father of our Lord Jesus Christ, the Father of compassion and the God of all comfort, who comforts us in all our troubles, so that we can comfort those in any trouble with the comfort we ourselves receive from God.

THOUGHTS TO CONSIDER

1. Have you experienced a profound loss in your life? To whom or what did you turn to for solace and comfort?
2. When you are sad, what do you do to make yourself feel better? Do you have music, a movie, or a friend to talk to that always makes you feel better?
3. How have you experienced His comfort and healing throughout your life?
4. How have you been a comforter to someone you know? If you don't feel as if you have been a comforter to someone, consider this: how can you comfort someone through a tough time?
5. Who do you know who could use a lift from you today? Would they enjoy a phone call, a visit, a meal or dessert you make and take to them, a letter or card? Don't wait—do something for them today!

A PRAYER FOR YOU

Abba, Father,

You tell us in Matthew 5, "Blessed are those who mourn, for they will be comforted." Right now, Father, bless those who suffer from loss, and the grief that inevitably follows. Come alongside them when they go through those hard times, providing Your comfort. Give them complete awareness of Your love and support for them in their darkness, knowing they are never alone, for You never leave or forsake us. The unfailing love of the Lord never changes. His mercies are new every morning.

Show those suffering in grief that new mercies will come. Fill them with the knowledge that in being a light to others, even as they still suffer, the darkness will begin to subside for them. By focusing on others in need, they, in turn, will again live fully in Your light. Though we suffer for a time, lifting others up ultimately lifts us up as well, and we begin to look forward to whatever joys You have in store. Abba, we rejoice as You deliver again beauty for ashes and oil of joy for mourning.

In Jesus' name we pray, amen.

ADDITIONAL SCRIPTURES ON COMFORT

Psalm 34:18, Lamentations 3:31-32, Psalm 94:19, Hebrews 4:16, 2 Corinthians 4:18, Romans 8:18, Revelation 21:4

THOUGHTS, PRAYERS, & CONVERSATIONS I NEED TO HAVE

_____

_____

_____

_____

_____

_____

_____

_____

_____

_____

_____

intimidation

BY ZATOYIA JONES-COLQUITT

Does a superwoman ever feel afraid, anxious, or intimidated? You tell me. I am a mother, an intercessor, a pastor's wife (which is a whole thing in and of itself), a friend, a teacher, a motivator, and an encourager. I have two master's degrees and a passion for helping others develop personally and professionally so that they can move to the next level in their lives. So how or when did I become afraid, anxious, or intimidated? Let me walk you through my story.

I first experienced intimidation moments before I gave a presentation on communication. I was nervous, sweating, and shaking. I had all my notes in front of me, but when it was time to speak, anxiety kicked in, and the words became blurry on the paper. All eyes were on me, and I could not see the 12-pitch, double-spaced notes typed in front of me. Fighting frustration, I had no other choice but to go by memory; but because I was nervous, I stumbled over my words and could not remember everything. Maybe I should have titled the presentation "How To Not Communicate When You Are Nervous". I imagined disappointment in everyone's eyes. All I could hear in my head was, "She is not making sense," and "She is doing a terrible job." Safe to say, that was not a pleasant experience for me, so I walked away from speaking.

A couple of years later, I found myself in a different position that required me to speak publicly again, and I finally felt ready. I had typed my notes in a twenty-point font, doubled-spaced, and even typed a few words in bold to remember the emphasis I wanted to add. I practiced memorizing my script for a month and a half, just in case. It's over. I did it! The crowd was moved by the words I spoke, but my inner critic's feedback was silence and blank stares. Intimidated and embarrassed, I backed down. In my head, all I could hear was that I wasn't good enough. I let those words haunt me to the point that I decided I was done with public speaking for good, but deep down, I knew I needed to get past this.

Scared, intimidated, and worried about what everyone else thought of me, I ran again. I decided I did not need that position. It was too uncomfortable. After all, I told myself that I worked better behind the scenes, making others look good. I was convinced I didn't need all that attention, but God was showing me visions of becoming a motivational speaker, speaking to large crowds of people. "For I know the plans I have for you," declares the Lord, "plans to prosper you and not to harm you, plans to give you hope and a future" (Jeremiah 29:11 NIV).

Now a a pastor and gospel artist's wife, a pastor's sister, and the daughter-in-law of a pastor and powerful prayer warrior who taught me how to intercede in prayer, I knew I had to stop running. But instead, I felt even more intimidated. I allowed fear and intimidation to lead me away from the prayer training. Now, my sister and friends are powerful prayer warriors like my mother-in-law, and I'm not. Full of disappointment, I regret how much time I spent running and making excuses. I wanted more, too. So, I cried out, "Father, help me. Stop me from running!" And God did just that! I knew I had a voice and I wanted to be who God called me to be.

He surrounded me with bold and powerful warriors who would work with me so that I didn't give up. They stood by me when I tried to run, prayed for me, developed a relationship with me, and showed me who God really is. When I talked to them about my fear, they shared how they, too, got nervous, but trusted God and relied on Him to use and speak through them. All I had to do was trust Him. By spending time in the Word, I developed a closer relationship with God. He continued to strengthen me, heal me, and restore my faith and trust in Him. The Bible says, "For God hath not given us the spirit of fear; but of power, and of love, and of a sound mind," (2 Timothy 1:7 KJV). After putting God first, I recognized that power, love, and soundness in my life. I no longer do it for everyone else, I do it for God. I am now teaching more, ministering more, and praying more independently and in a crowd! I may have taken baby steps to get here, but I am no longer running. I walk by faith and trust that He will walk with me and see me through each stage of my life, even when I am afraid. Why don't you join me and do the same? Stop comparing yourself to other people! Stop running from your purpose!

2 TIMOTHY 1:7 NIV

For the Spirit God gave us does not make us timid, but gives us power, love and self-discipline.

THOUGHTS TO CONSIDER

1. Are you running from your purpose?
2. Do you feel you're not good enough?
3. Do you compare yourself to others?

A PRAYER FOR YOU

Father God,

Thank You for standing by me and never giving up on me. Thank You for building confidence in me and helping me face my fear. I know I can't do this without You. Help me to continue to trust in You and rely on Your direction and guidance to see me through the fearful times, the intimidating times, and the times I am afraid. Give me the boldness to do what You have called me to do. Help me stay focused on You and I will forever give You all the glory, honor, acknowledgment, and praise.

In Christ Jesus' mighty and precious name, amen!

ADDITIONAL SCRIPTURES ON BOLDNESS

Acts 4:31, Hebrews 12:1-2, Galatians 2:20, 2 Timothy 2:15, 1 John 4:18, Hebrews 13:6, 2 Corinthians 3:12

THOUGHTS, PRAYERS, & CONVERSATIONS I NEED TO HAVE

_____

_____

_____

_____

_____

_____

_____

_____

worry

BY ALLMA JOHNSON

Have you ever been fearful? Have you been overwhelmed and said, "What should I do?" Have you ever said, "I did not sign up for this!"?

Well, I can say yes to all three of those statements. I would like to share about a season in my life where fear was so strong and bold, it blinded me like a thick fog. I could not see anything else, only fear. I faced my father being diagnosed with an accelerated form of Dementia brought on by Alzheimer's Disease. The signs of his diseases were so subtle that no one knew he was suffering.

This season in my life came wrapped in a huge, UGLY bow-tied box, with a card signed by uncertainty attached. I remember being so absorbed by my circumstance that I said aloud, "I did not sign up for this!"

In my fear, I asked God, "What is happening, Lord?" and "How am I supposed to do this during a pandemic?" At that moment, I realized I was letting my situation affect my understanding of who God was. Although I was upset and fearful, when I asked, Jesus answered, showing me the quietness of His love.

When I arrived at my father's house, I wondered what I should do. I wondered where the light at the end of the tunnel that everyone talks about was. I'll be the first to tell you that I did not see it! There, while I held the key to the house, I began asking questions of God.

God reminded me of Psalms 94:9—a verse He originally showed me during another trial in 2018. "Can the one who shaped the ear not hear, the one who formed the eye not see?" As soon as I answered these two questions with a resounding "Yes," my anxiety dissipated. I realized that Jesus was with me just like He was with the disciples in the storm when the wind and the waves obeyed Him.

Jesus tells us in His Word not to fear because He goes before us, He will be with us, and He will never leave or abandon us. We should never be afraid or discouraged.

My first desire was to please Jesus in everything, so I did this by honoring my father. Gone were the emotions I carried about not meeting my father until I was twenty-seven years old. Gone was the regret of time that had been stolen from me. My greatest desire was to honor God and His Word, which says to "Honor your father and your mother."

When I began caring for my father, I cried daily. I cried tears of fear, loss, and hurt. I cried tears of the unknown. I cried tears out of love for him, although he could not comprehend the love I showed. I loved him because he is my dad.

During that time, I did not realize that God had been showing me the quietness of His love all along. His covering over us is never-ending. Through my pain, I was comforted. I prayed and professed God's Word aloud, and as I did, fear drowned. Some love loud while others love quietly. In this season of my life, Jesus showed me loudly the quietness of His love.

I became overwhelmed feeling God's love and learned that in silence, Jesus IS! God moving in my situation was so profound. I became more at peace with what I faced. Even with stumbling blocks, His silence broke barriers and spoke louder than the chaos around me. Although I complained before, I refused to complain about this, because God showed me again that He triumphs in all things.

I learned in the quietness of Jesus' love, He first had to be my portion, and portion is love. Hannah, whom we read about in 1 Samuel, knew what it meant to live with God as her portion, but she had to learn how to invite Him into that space first. We all learn our greatest lessons by trusting God through difficult times, and Hannah was no exception. From her story, we discover a deeper trust in the One who is above all in the scariest times. Even when we feel like we are not enough, we do not have enough, and we want to scream, "Enough is enough," we learn what it means when God is our portion.

In the quietness of Jesus' love, we need to look ahead — while giving God total praise—because instead of us having it all together, it is God who holds all things together. So, what should we fear? Absolutely nothing! Jesus' perfect love casts out all fear, and we know that we are in His perfect will for our lives when we honor Him.

In times of fear and worry, remember to open your heart to Jesus and bask in the quietness of His love. Allow His presence to quiet your heart. We cannot have peace if our hearts and minds are agitated, going a hundred miles per hour. Worship Jesus and rest in the quietness of His love!

Now, ask yourself these questions. In what area of my life have I withheld trust in God? Have I invited Jesus into my space as my portion? In what area of my life have I been struggling with fear, letting go, and surrendering all to Jesus? Do I profess the Word of God daily?

I hope that by being open and sharing my heart, I have encouraged you to never fear. I encourage you to give Jesus your fear. I encourage you to surrender all to Jesus!

PSALM 94:9 NIV

Does he who fashioned the ear not hear?
Does he who formed the eye not see?

THOUGHTS TO CONSIDER

1. When was the last time you were quiet before the Lord?

2. What does your private prayer time look like?

3. Is there a space where you can get away to spend time with the Lord in your home?

4. How can you invite your children and your family into your quiet time?

A PRAYER FOR YOU

Dear Lord Jesus,

Thank You that Your love that is patient, kind, and does not boast; it is not proud and it is not rude or self-seeking. Your love, Lord Jesus, is not easily angered and keeps no record of wrongs. The love You have for us, Jesus, does not delight in evil, but rejoices with the truth. The love of You, Lord, always protects, always trusts, always hopes, and always preserves. Lord, thank You that in Your love, You quiet our hearts and minds, and silence all those confusing voices and sounds of fear. Let the quietness of Your love permeate us like never before and rest upon our hearts and minds like boulders. Because You first loved us, I rejoice that I can securely rest in the quietness of Your love.

In Jesus' name, amen!

ADDITIONAL SCRIPTURES ON RESTING IN THE LORD

Psalm 127:2, Exodus 33:14, Psalm 46:10, Matthew 11:28-30, Jeremiah 17:8, Hebrews 4:9-10, 1 John 4:4, 1 Corinthians 2:9

THOUGHTS, PRAYERS, & CONVERSATIONS
I NEED TO HAVE

_____

_____

_____

_____

_____

_____

_____

_____

_____

_____

a prayer for your heart

Dear Jesus,

I want to experience the freedom, the joy, the beauty, and the peace that I've discovered through the pages of this book for myself. It is my prayer that You will come into my heart and strengthen my faith in Your perfect presence every day. I ask for Your forgiveness. Save me from my sins and draw me closer to You, Jesus. I trust with You my past, my present, and my future. Thank You for saving me, healing me, and restoring me. I dedicate my story to You for Your glory.

In Your precious and holy name, Jesus, I pray, amen!

acknowledgements

Anthologies are incredibly sensitive and delicate pieces of art-work. Authors join them as an act of a trust.

To the twenty-one women who have helped to write this book, thank you. You trusted in my ability to hear God's voice and uphold His standard of excellence. You trusted the people who would join this journey and the story we would tell, al-though you didn't know them. You trusted my ability to main-tain the authenticity of your voice and the heart with which you've written. You trusted in my ability to weave your story together with the others' through the content, structure, and edi-torial process. I am so grateful that you owned this opportunity from the onset. You helped lead meetings, facilitated panels, and marketed this book with enthusiasm. It is my prayer that I have honored your deepest wishes.

To the authors of Just Believe: Every Summer Has A Story, Desiree and Christine, I do not have words to thank you for how much time you spent pouring over this manuscript with me. It's always incredibly humbling when someone comes along with as much passion and care as you have. As I think back to that first real conversation we had at the Barnes and Noble, I am even more astounded by the strategic God we serve. I can't believe He had this in mind when we met there. Ladies, it's my prayer that I can show up for you as you've shown up for me.

Natasha, the interviews and our book release party would not have even been successful had you not stepped in and taken ownership of them, and I am grateful.

Mom, Ms. Denise Lane, Jacque Harris-Smith, Arnette Coleman, Sheila Weathers, and Christian Cashelle, thank you for reviewing the earliest versions of our submissions and for contributing to the conversations that led us to develop this book.

I knew that I wanted to invite other successful authors into this process to help our authors grow, even before we hosted the author interest meeting. I just didn't know who you would be until God shined a spotlight on you. Christian Cashelle, Cassie Edwards-Whitlow, Desiree Micheels, and Christine Prato-Coleman, thank you for your selflessness. You helped to bring us together and I honor you for your choice to share how much you have learned during your time authoring books and working in the publishing industry. I know those lessons did not come easy or cheap, but you have been so gracious, and I pray your writing careers continue to bless the Kingdom of God as God continues to bless you with new levels of influence and support.

Dr. Parson, thank you for writing our foreword with an incredibly tight timeline. I honor and admire your work in every way. I am becoming the leader I am today because of the leader you've been in my life. It's my prayer I can add value to you in new ways. I'm trusting God to give you the desires of your heart because you have served tirelessly in our communities through the work you've committed yourself to in psychology, ministry, and education.

The board and the volunteer team for The Colorfully Candid Paradigm, Incorporated support the very foundation of the work we do. Mom, Jacque, Arnette, and Tina, we have proof that where two or three are gathered in His name, there He is, as we're told in Matthew 18:20. I bless God for your heart for this ministry, the time and money you've poured into it, and your belief that our work is important.

Most of all to my beloved Savior, to the God who is able to do exceedingly abundantly beyond all that I could ask or think, according to the power working in me as it says in the King James Version of Ephesians 3:20, I give you all the glory for the vision, the project, and the execution. You are my reward, and I marvel at how You've been with me during every part of this process. I can't thank You enough for the opportunity and the privilege.

The Colorfully Candid Paradigm, Incorporated was founded by Liv Dooley and Beverly Young in 2014. The mission of The Colorfully Candid Paradigm is to enhance the emotional intelligence of young ladies, ages 11-18, and their families throughout underserved communities by equipping participants with the tools to effectively handle stress and to succeed in life. Together, with a variety of incredible women throughout the local Las Vegas area, where the organization was founded, and beyond, we host programming for moms, mentors, and daughters. Our programming includes book clubs for girls in middle and high school, scholarship opportunities, meet ups for women, and conferences for girls and women of every generation. We are intent on finding our value in Christ Jesus, creating community among women and girls, and elevating Christ's love through candid conversations. For information on how to found a Colorfully Candid charter in your city, please visit www.colorfullycandid.org.

CPSIA information can be obtained
at www.ICGtesting.com
Printed in the USA
LVHW021255250920
667085LV00004B/260